Introduction

I couldn't believe it! There I was in the British Museum in London, a thousand miles from home, and several thousand years in the past. I was in the collection of ancient Egypt looking at the mummies, art, and other wonderful things when I saw a doll that looked like it could have been made by a mountain craftsman. The arms were jointed in a way that was almost identical to the Dancing Sams and other toys that I grew up with as a child and that are still delighting children today.

Until then I didn't realize how old an idea jointed figures are, but it is easy to understand why. They can move! You can mold them and shape them to take hundreds of positions and attitudes. They will fit almost any story your imagination can make up, and when the story moves so do they!

The Santas in this book are in that tradition. Some are loose enough to dance on a paddle board like Dancing Sam, when someone taps it to the tune of "Rudolph the Red-nosed Reindeer." Others will stand on their own or sit in a sleigh full of presents. All of them are sure to delight.

A Word About Knives

A lot of people ask me about the knives I use for carving. Since I make my living with them, they are very important to me.

Of course a carver can use just about any old knife if they want to bad enough. When I started carving I used a pocket knife. Old man Cowdan in Gatlinburg, Tennessee used to make a knife that just fit the palm of the hand perfectly. He wanted to give me a knife, but I told him I just as soon use my pocket knife. He told me to go home and put the pocket knife in a drawer for two weeks while I used his knife. In two weeks try to use it again. He said he bet I'd take the pocket knife and throw it in the crick. Will he came by a few weeks later and saw me using his knife. "Where's your pocket knife?" he asked. "In the crick" I said with a smile.

While a pocket knife is just fine for a casual carver, when you get serious about the craft, it's important to get some serious tools. I like my knife to have a large handle because it gives me a lot of leverage. The length of the handle gives you more reach, and the straightness means you cut away or toward yourself and still feel comfortable. The octagon shape allows you get a feel for the position of the blade. The bigness also helps eliminate the problem of the tool slipping out of your hand. A carving knife is primarily a tool. It's like the pickup truck. Everyone wants a truck to look nice, but the best truck is one that can do the job. This knife can.

The large, octagon shaped handle I like.

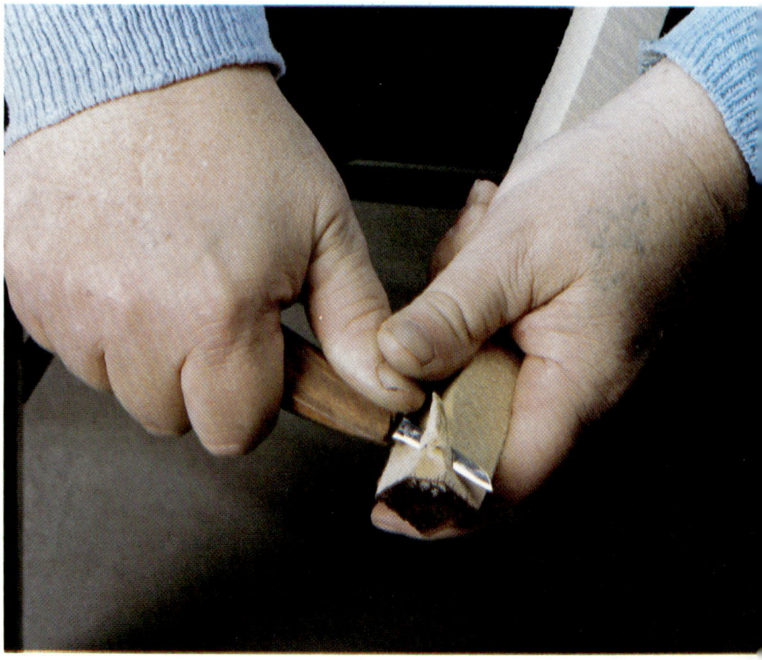

The leverage from the handle makes power cuts like this almost effortless.

Tom Wolfe Carves

Jointed Santas

Schiffer Publishing Ltd
77 Lower Valley Road, Atglen, PA 19310

Text written with and photography by Douglas Congdon-Martin

Contents

Designed by Bonnie Hensley

Library of Congress Catalog Number: 93-85230.

Printed in the United States of America.
ISBN: 0-88740-539-8

Published by Schiffer Publishing, Ltd.
77 Lower Valley Road
Atglen, PA 19310
Please write for a free catalog.
This book may be purchased from the publisher.
Please include $2.95 postage.
Try your bookstore first.

We are interested in hearing from authors
with book ideas on related subjects.

Even without the pressure of the second thumb, this is an easy cut.

The long handle also allows a much longer reach. The curved blade, used for cutting the inside of things, also does well on these long, power cuts. Note the position of the thumb.

For finer work the extra handle just sticks out the back of your fist.

Jointed Santa

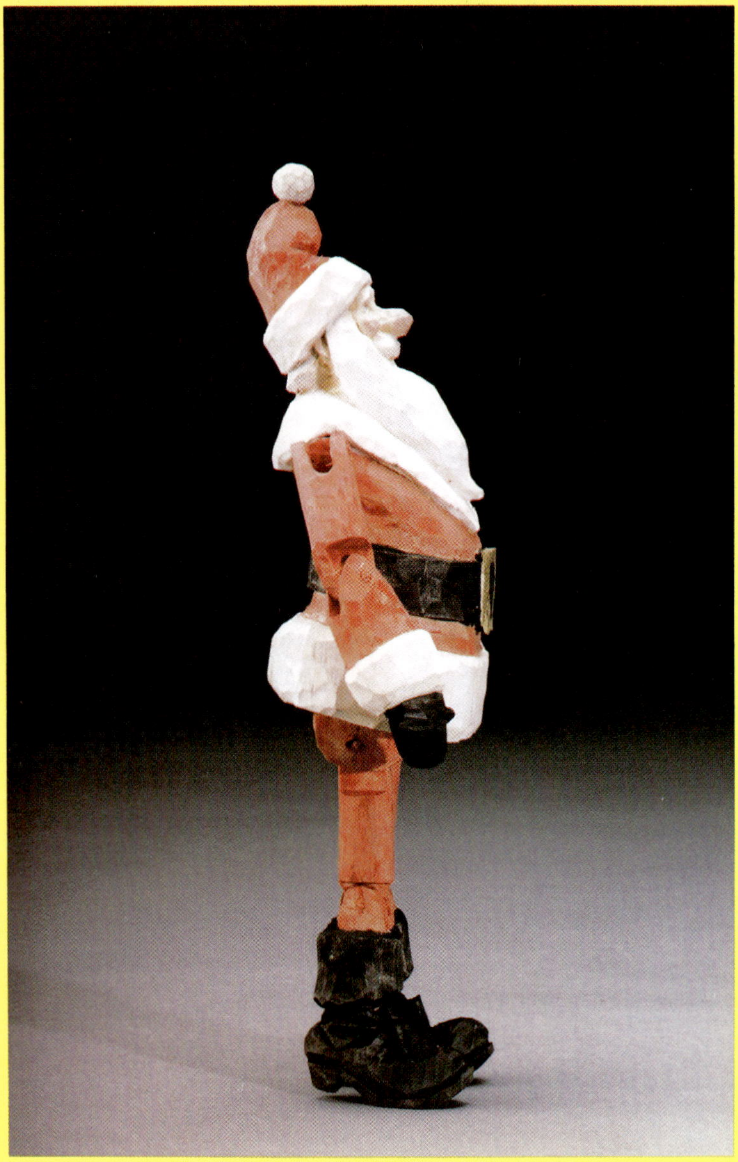

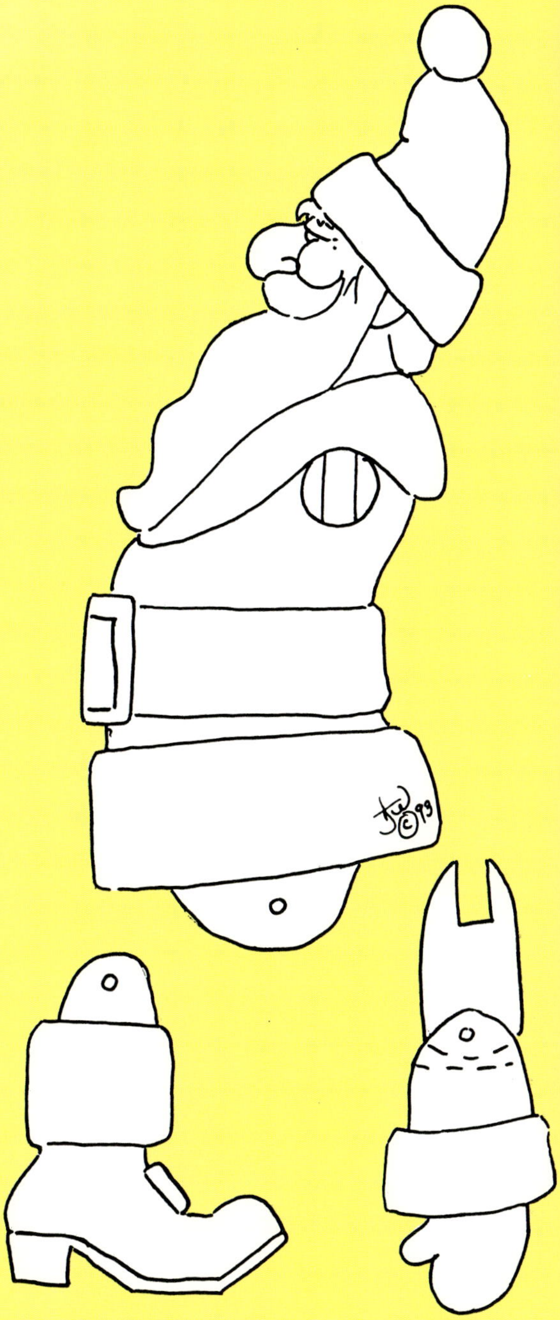

The pattern is shown at 66% of its actual size. If you wish to restore it to its original size, photocopy at 150%.

Carving the Jointed Santa

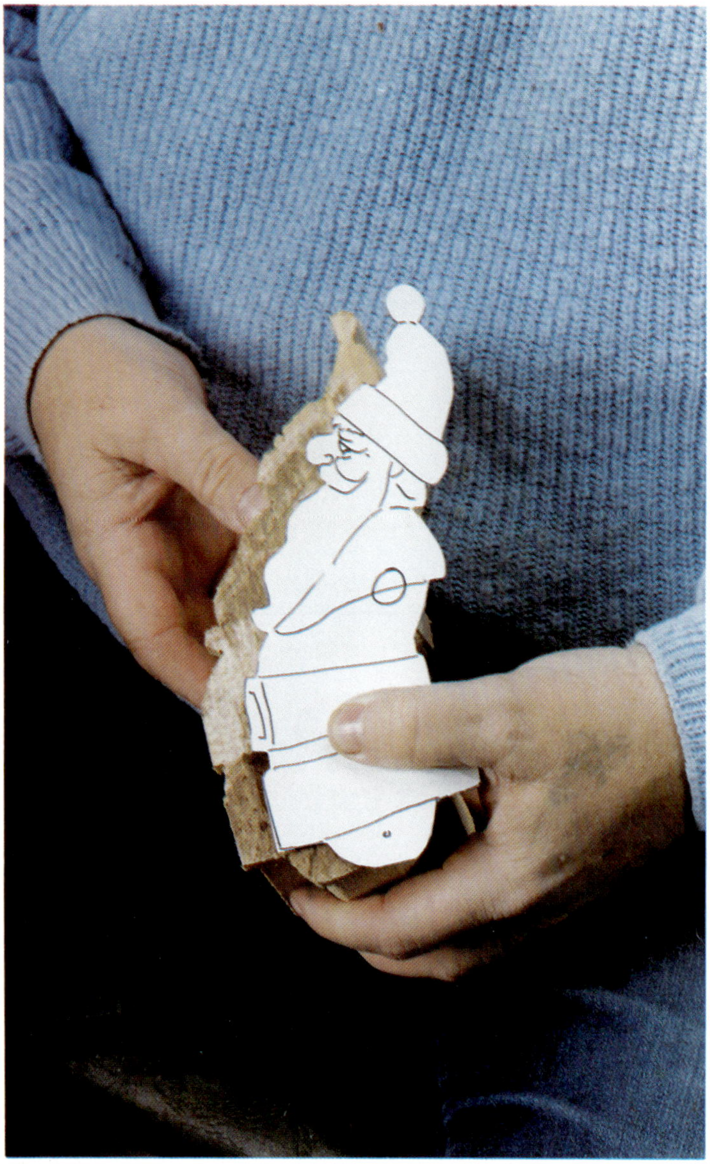

Trace the body pattern on a piece of 4 inch stock, and cut out on the band saw.

Cut off about a quarter inch on each side. Not only does this bring the piece to the right size, it also gets rid of some dirty wood which may dull your knife.

Drill a half-inch hole where the arm will go through the body.

Draw in the collar line and mark the area of the head to be removed.

At each of the four corners where the collar meets the head, use a rocking motion to cut a stop.

Mark the center all the way around the body.

Trim back to it. Do the back first...

On the front and back mark the area to be removed from the side of the head.

then repeat the process on the front corners. First cut the stop...

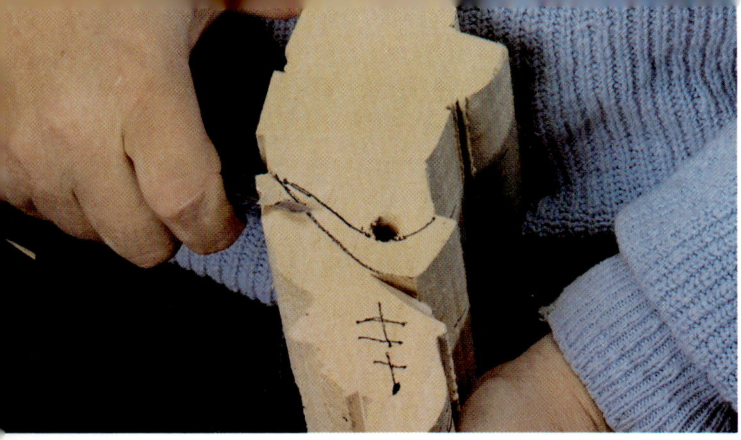

then trim back to it.

Deepen the corners to the correct depth.

Cut a stop along the collar using either a knife with a turned down blade or one with a flat blade.

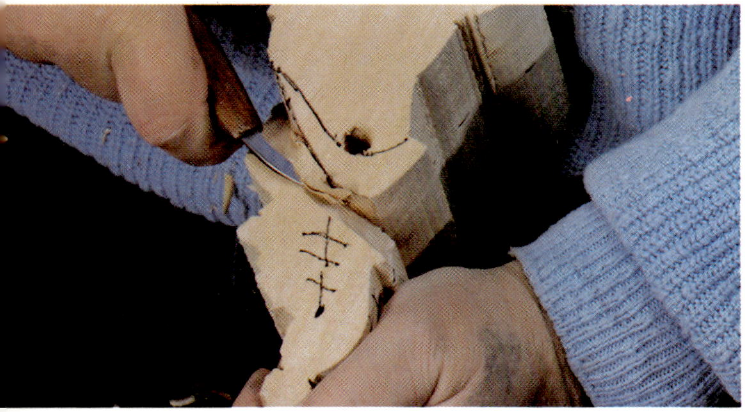

Cut back to it from the head.

Work up from the neck and chip off the excess wood at the sides of the head.

When the head is trimmed, mark the ball of the cap...

and the line of its peak.

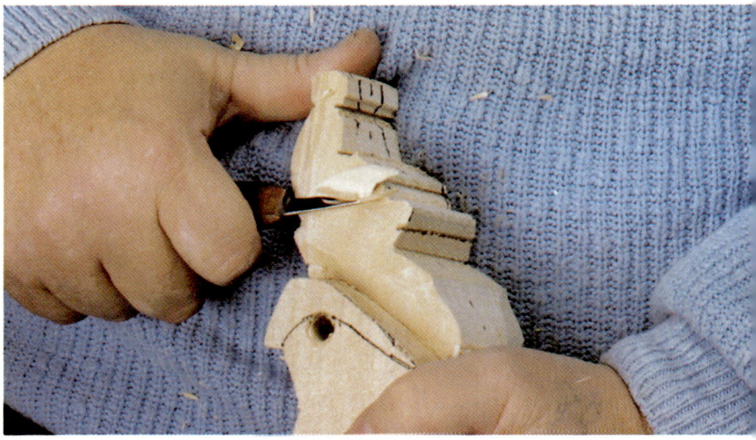

Trim it down to shape.

At this point I can see that the sides are not quite symmetrical. I use my finger and a pen as a depth gauge...

and transfer the difference to the other side to mark the area to be removed.

Cut away the excess.

Keep trimming to get the general shape, but keep it square for now. I find it easier to keep things proportional if I go to square before rounding things off.

Progress report.

Mark the width of the nose.

Use a small half-round gouge to remove the area beside the nose.

Finish it off with a knife.

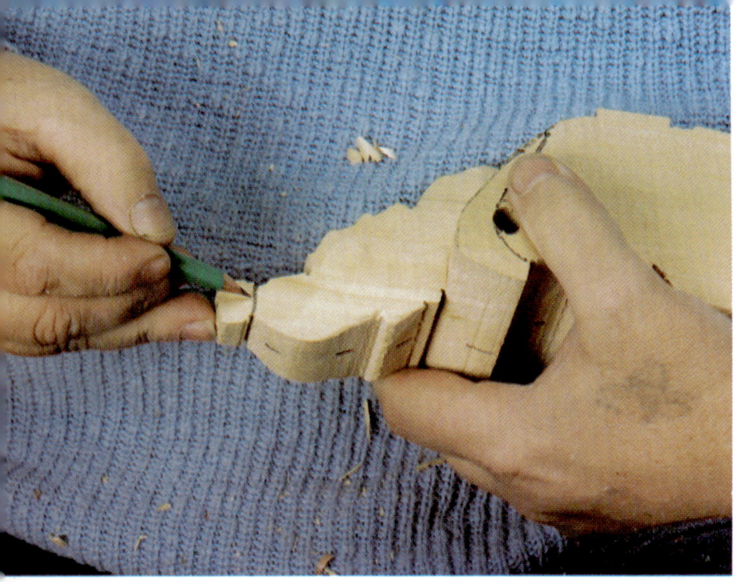

Mark the ball of the cap...

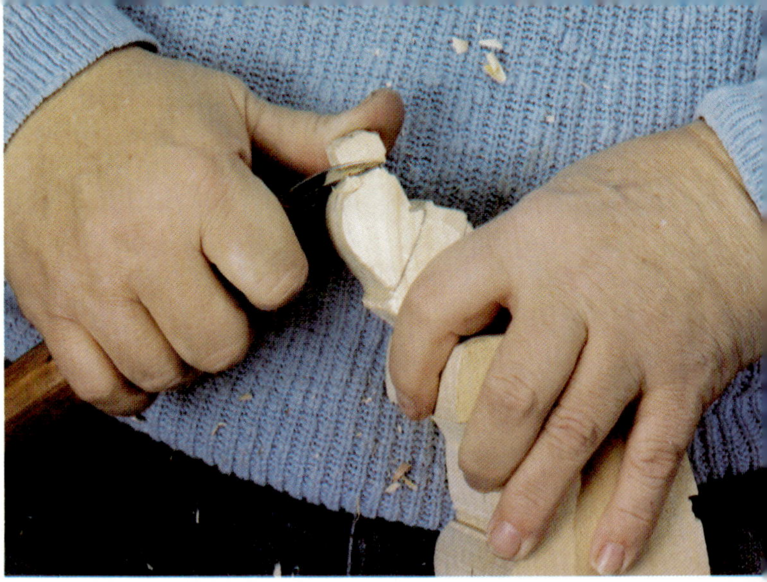

and back to it from the ball.

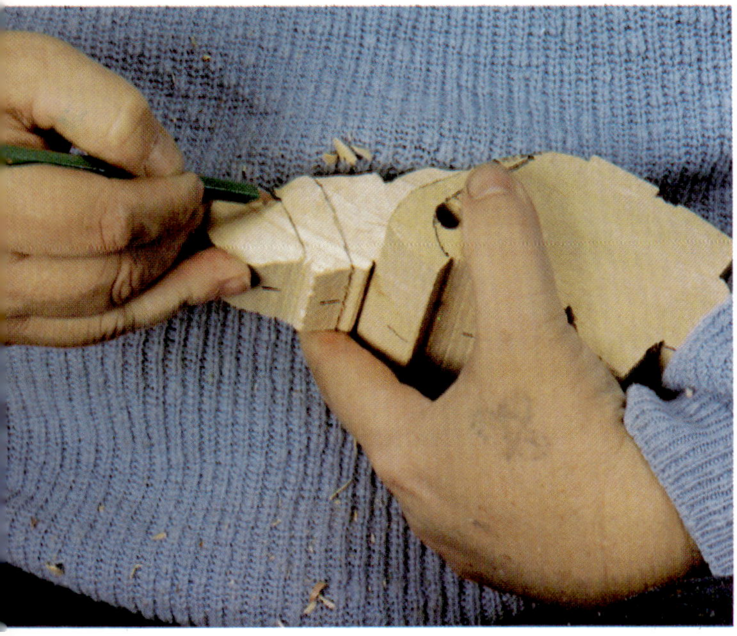

and its fur trim.

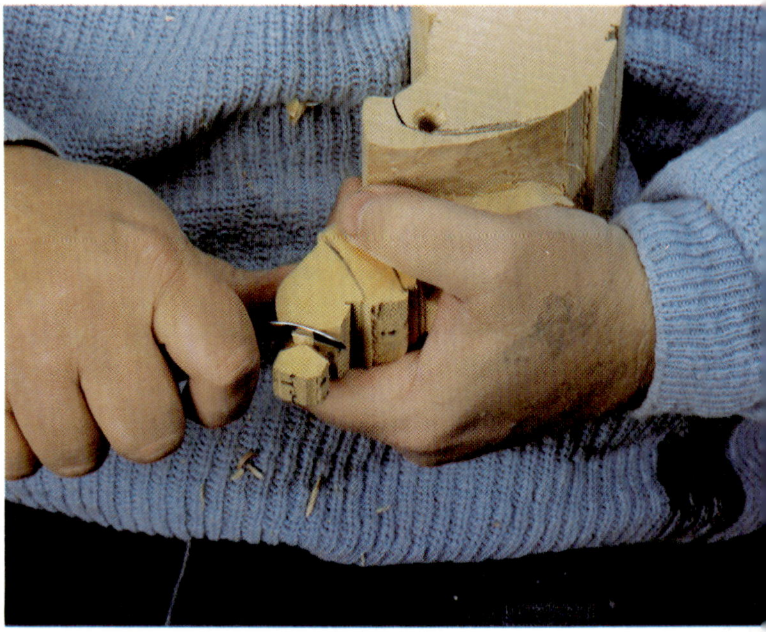

Do the same at the middle points.

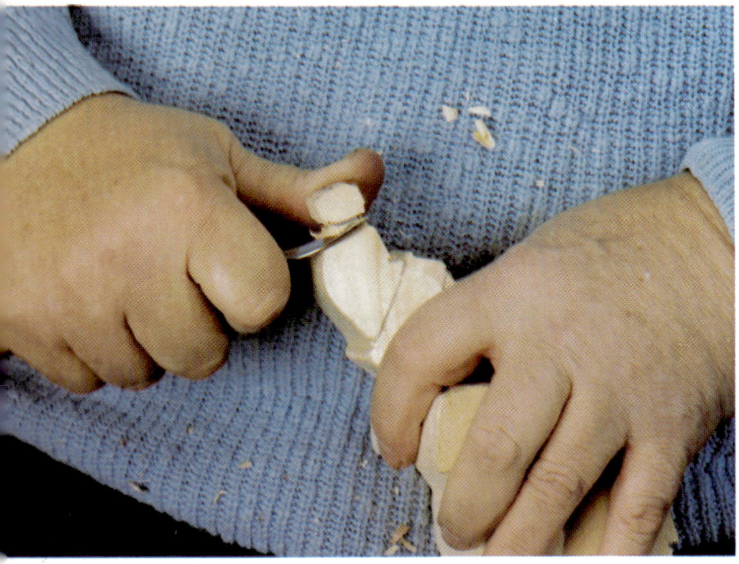

At the corners of the ball, cut in with a stop...

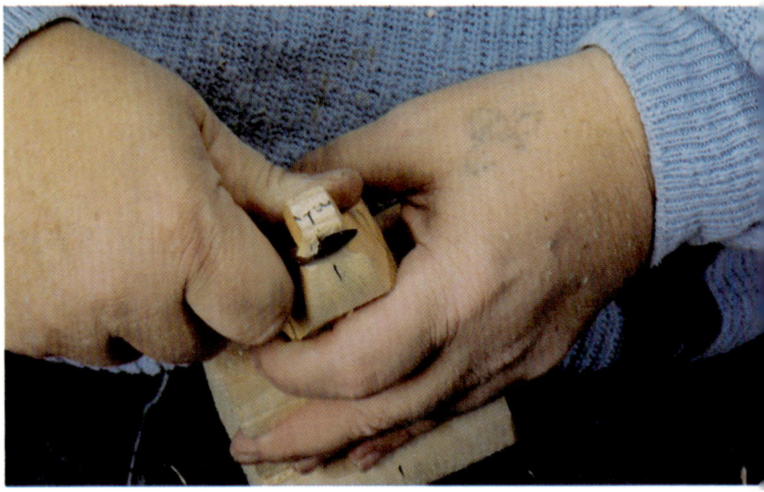

When you've cut all around the base of the ball, knock off the corners. Taking it to octagon before going to round helps keep the work symmetrical.

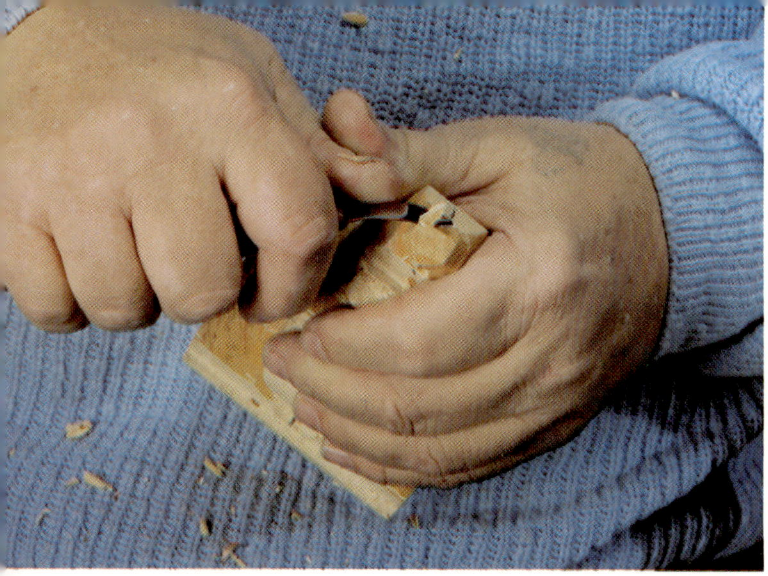

Round off the ball.

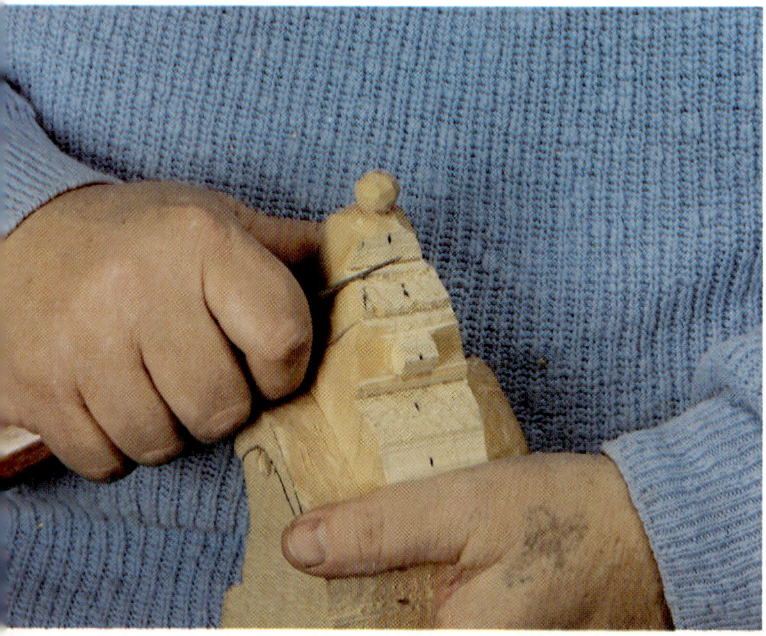

Where the cap meets the fur trim cut a stop on each corner

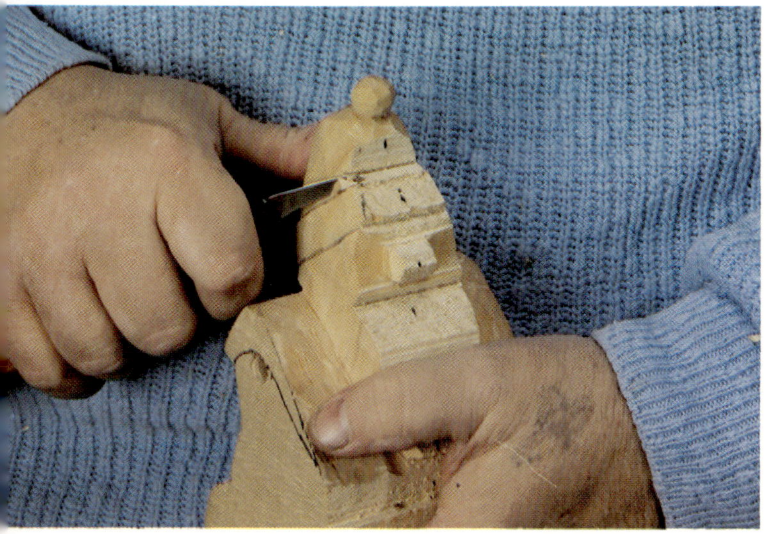

and cut back to it from the cap.

Do the same on the bottom edge of the trim, cutting a stop and trimming back to it from the face.

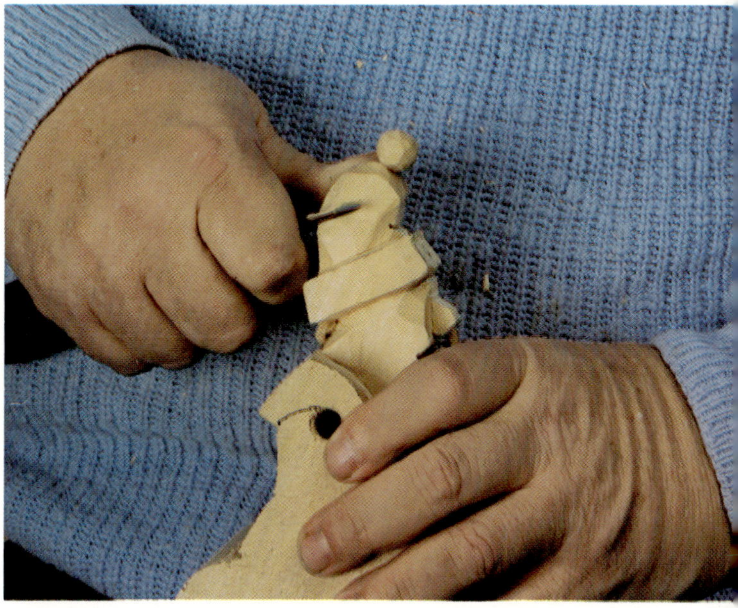

When the trim is defined, go back and knock the corners off the peak of the cap.

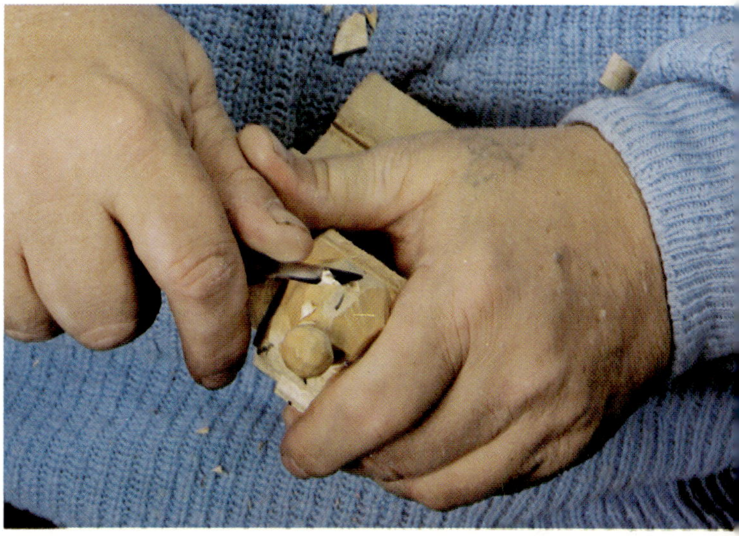

After getting to octagonal go back and round it off.

Knock off the corners of the fur trim...

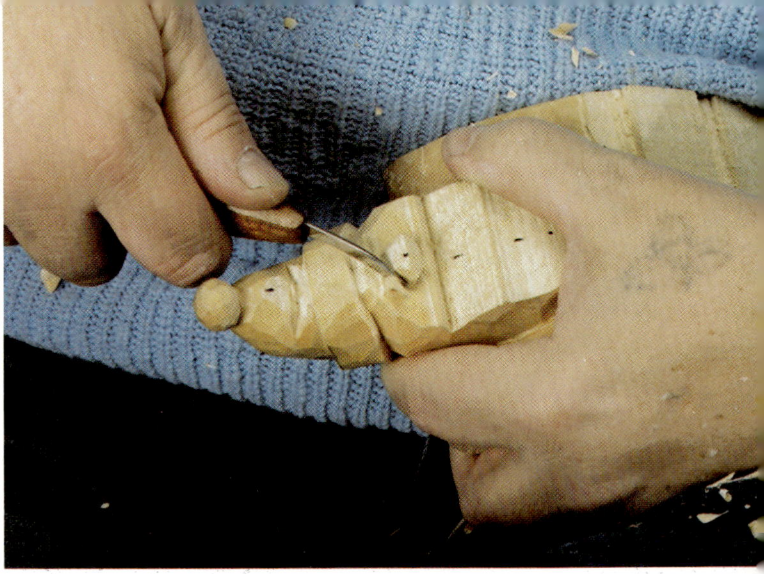

Make a similar cut at the top of the nose to create the bridge.

and go back and round it.

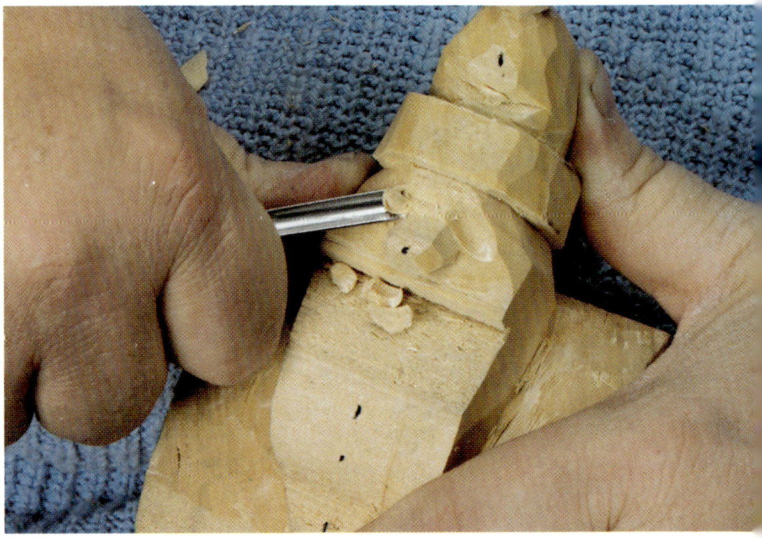

Come in from the outside with a gouge to create the eyesockets. Note the position of the thumb of the knife hand. It acts as a stop to keep you from going too far.

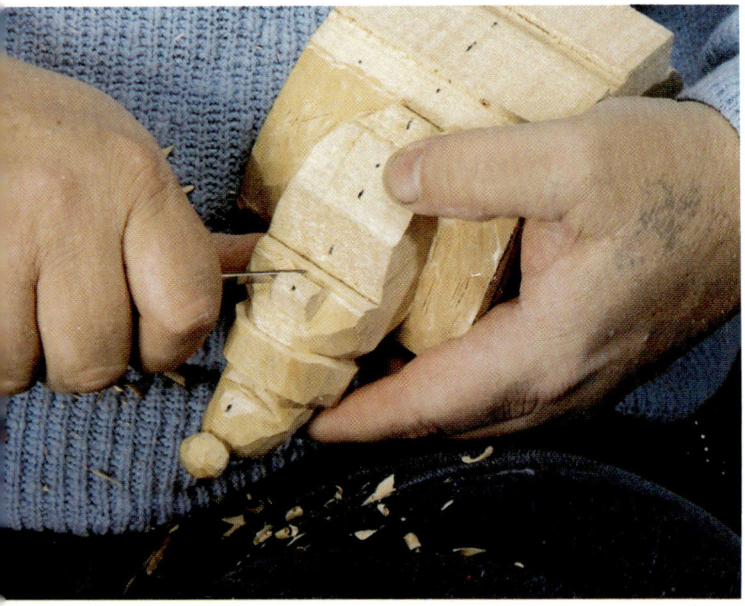

Cut at a 45 degree angle at the bottom corners of the nose to create an area for the nostrils.

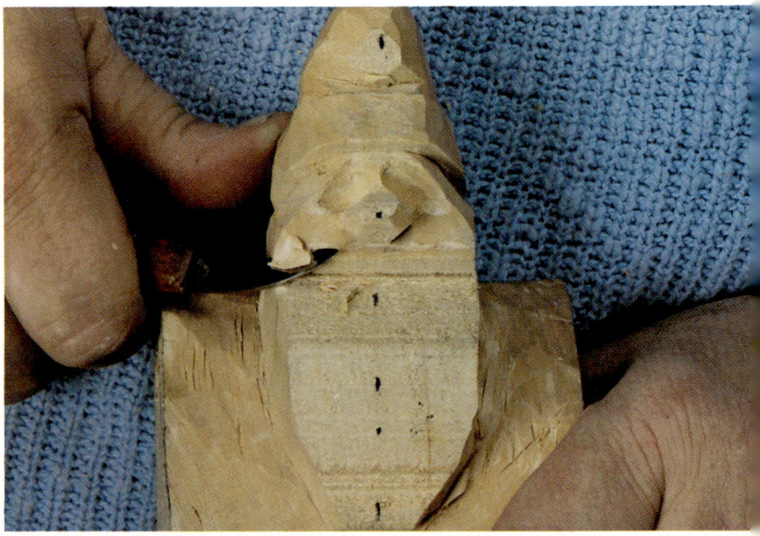

Knock off the corners of the face. This will keep you from the tendency to create a flat face.

Be sure to include the beard.

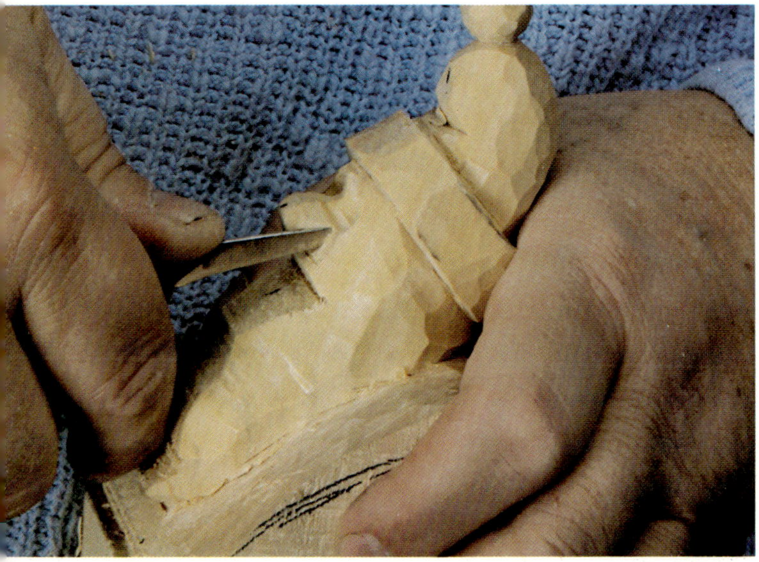

To create the line of the cheek, cut a stop along the nostril.

Cut in and down at a 45 degree angles along the cheek line...

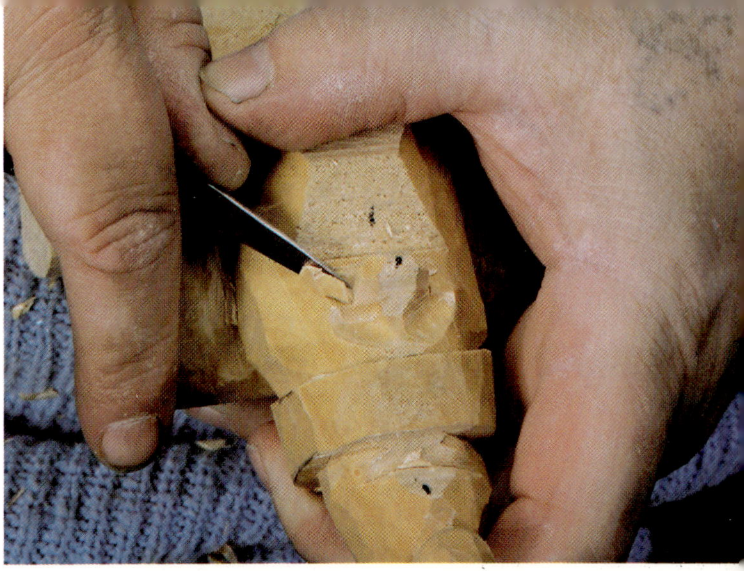

and cut up from the lip to pop out the nitch. If it doesn't pop out repeat the process until it does. Don't pick it out.

At this point you can see the possibilities for different characters by turning the moustache up or down or whatever.

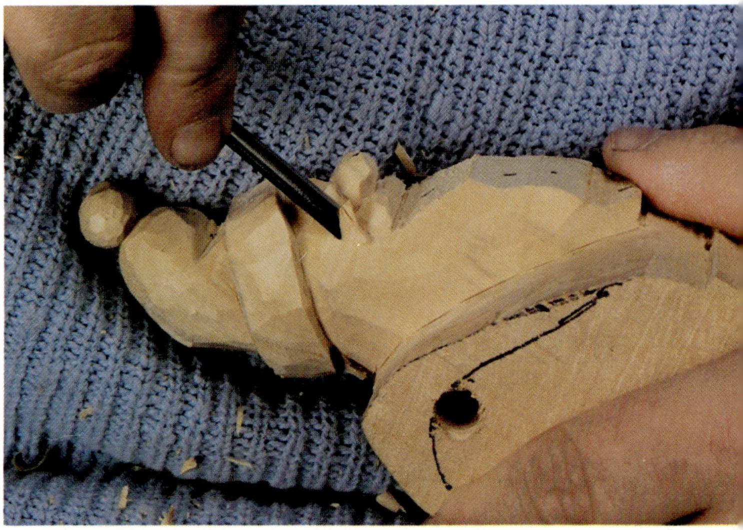

Use a flatter gouge with the cup side down to shape the cheek.

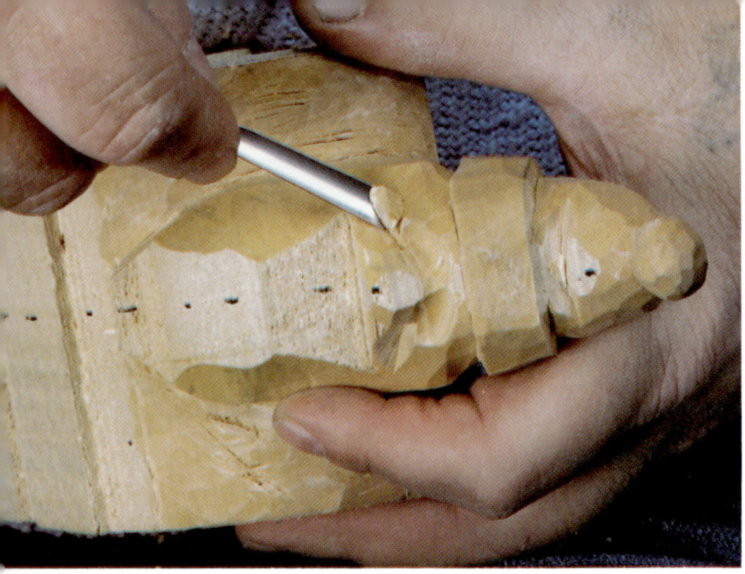

With the cup side up come up to the cut to trim it off.

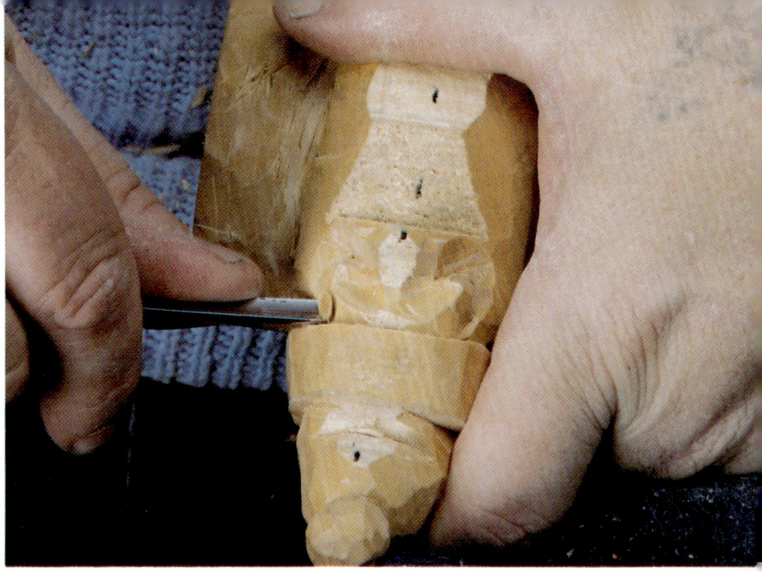

Trim it off at the line of the sideburn.

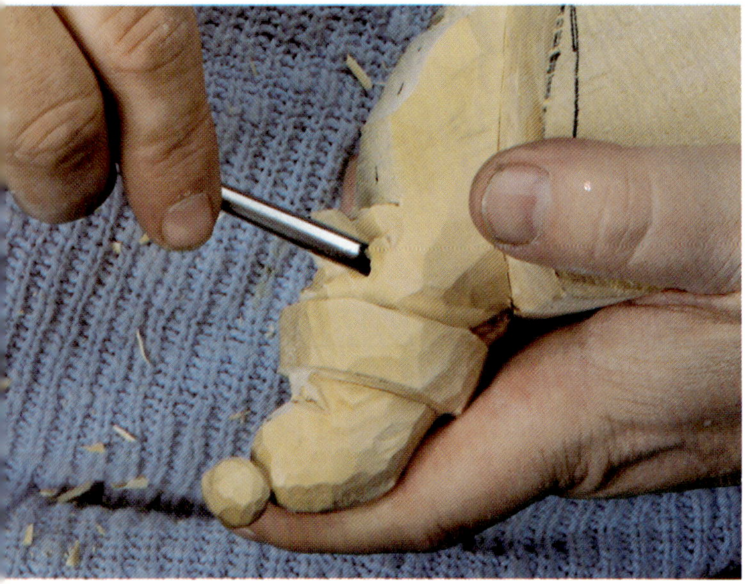

Continue around the side of the cheek using the same method.

Create a stop along the turned-up bottom edge of the moustache by pushing the gouge straight in. The sweep of the chisel helps keeps the side of the moustache symmetrical.

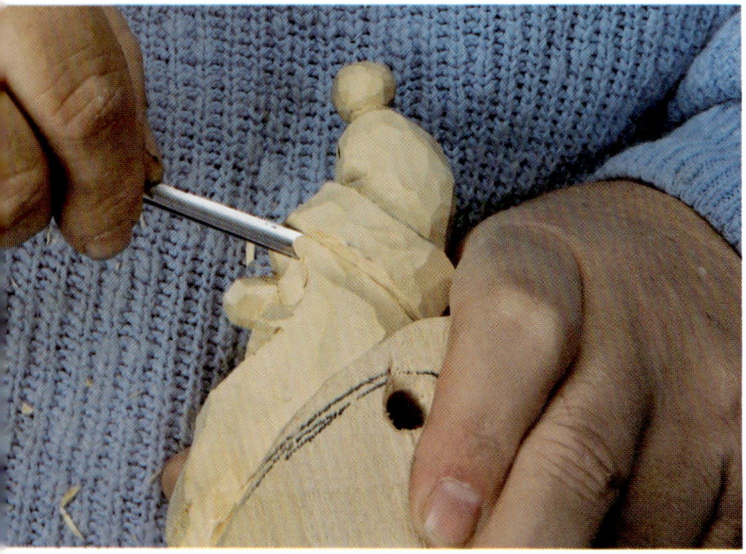

Come into the temple with the cup side of the gouge facing out.

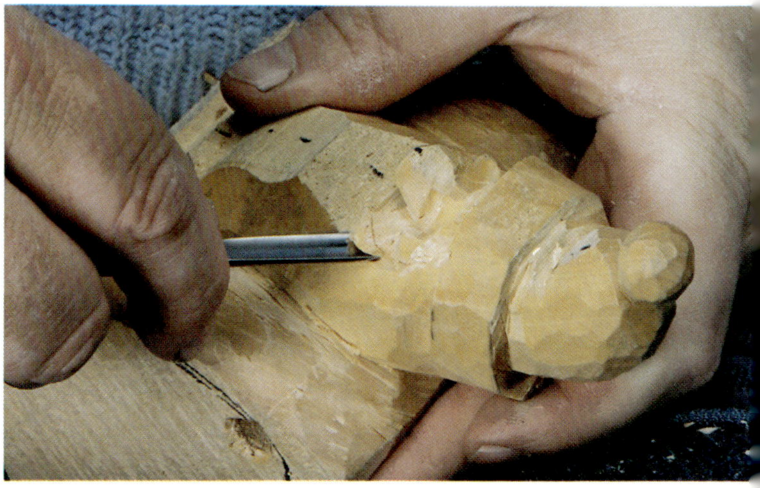

Come back to the stop from the beard to define the moustache.

Create the part of the moustache with the knife, cutting straight in on one side...

This hand and knife position make the curved cut easy.

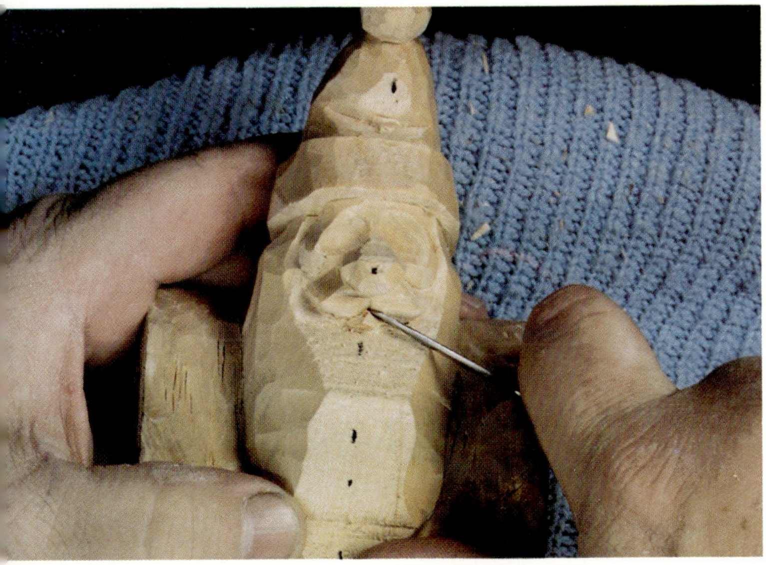

and the other to pop out a little wedge.

Trim away some of the beard on each side of the mouth to insinuate that there is a chin underneath it.

Progress on the head.

The shoulders need to be narrowed, so I mark the area to be removed. Be sure to continue the lines around to the back.

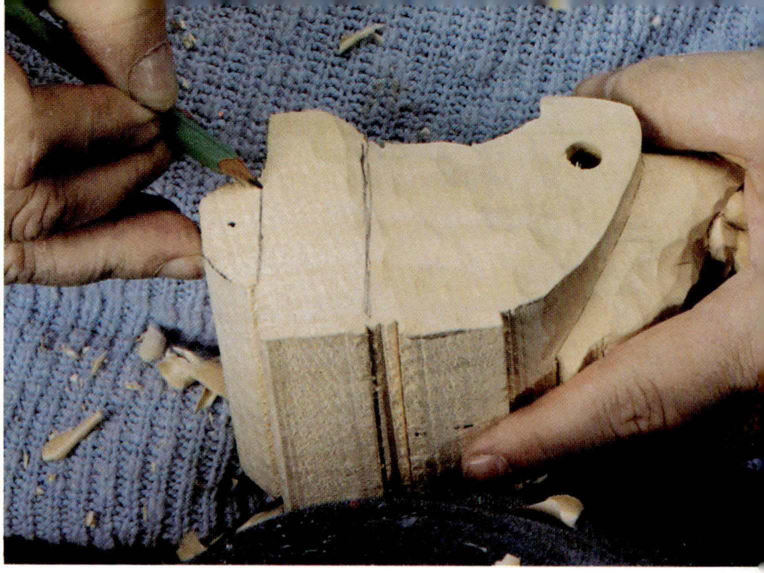

Mark the fur trim of the coat.

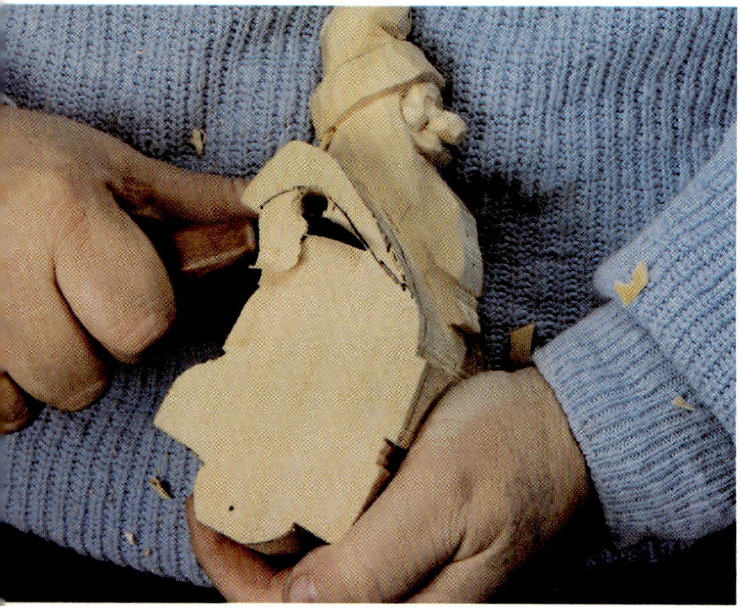

Use a knife to pop off the area to be removed.

Like we did on the cap, cut a stop at each corner...

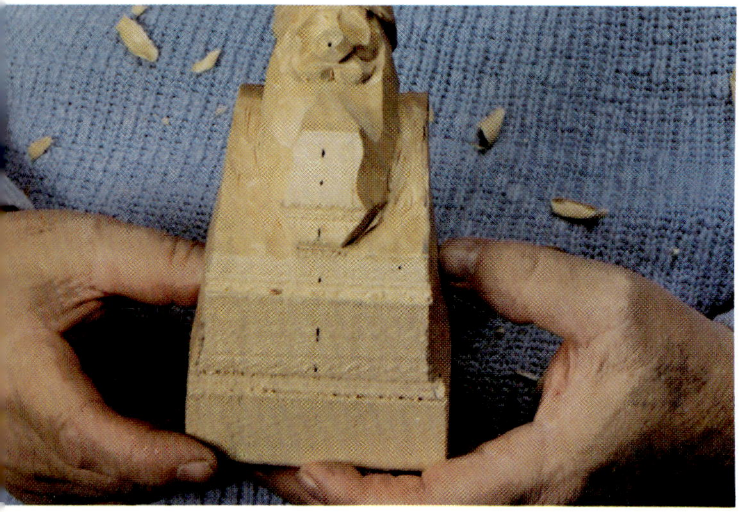

The result.

and trim back to it from the jacket.

Continue up the front corners of the coat

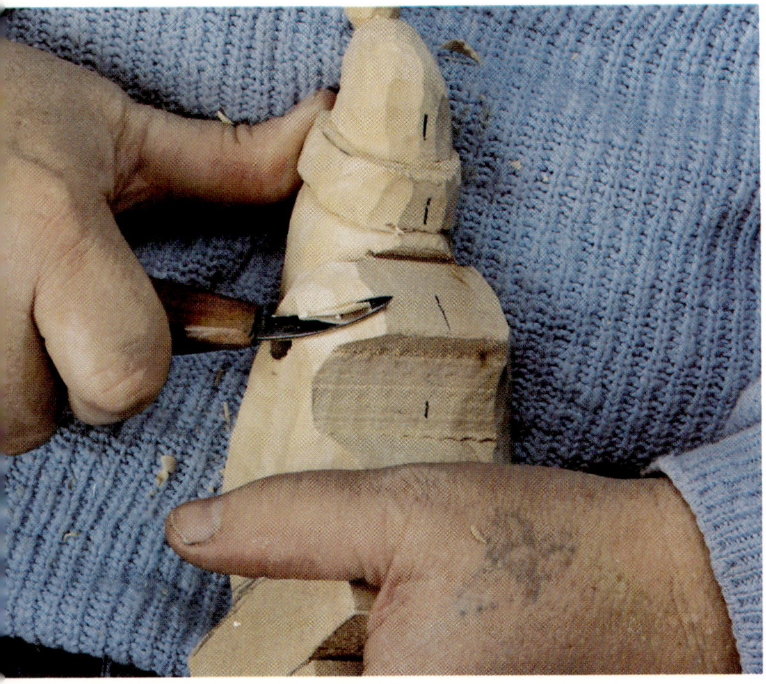

Do the same on the back corners.

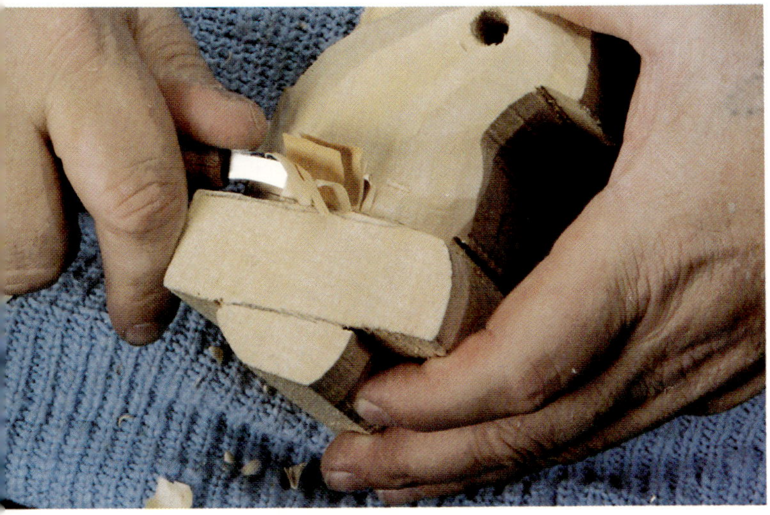

Round the sides, bringing out the fur trim as you do.

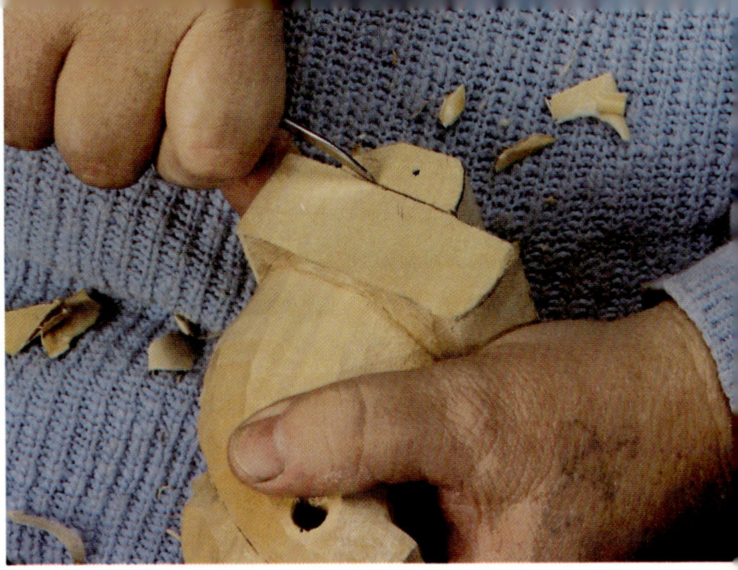

Cut a stop in line at the bottom of the trim, above the rump area where the legs will be attached.

Trim back to it from the rump until it comes in from the edge of the trim about as much as the coat does.

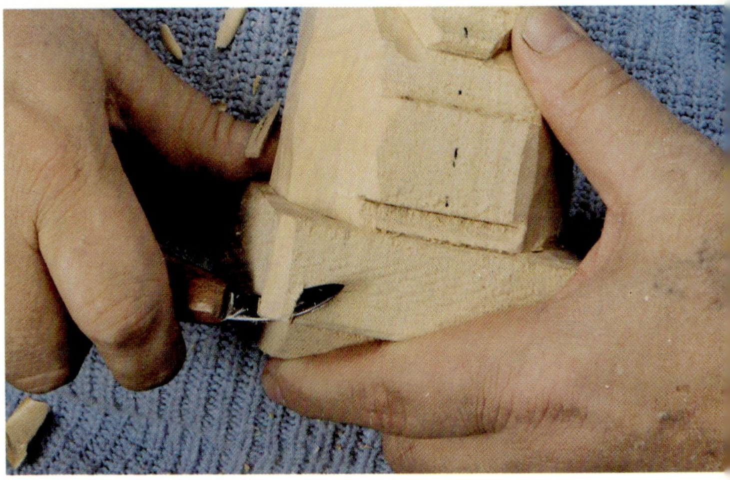

Knock the corners off the trim, taking it to octagonal.

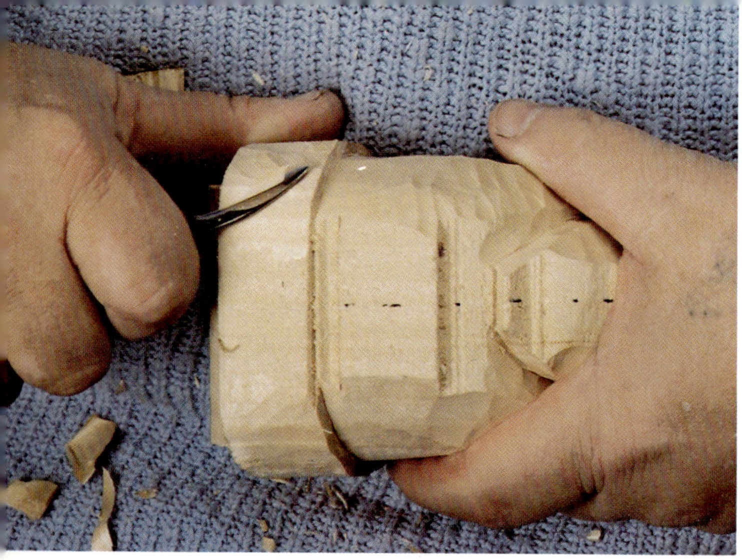

Go back and round the trim...

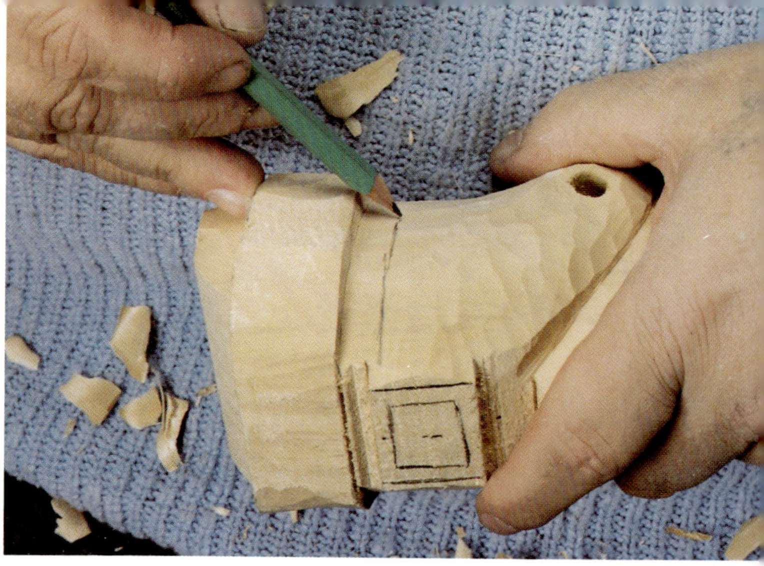

and the belt. A finger running along the bottom of the trim as you draw acts as a depth gauge to help the belt run parallel.

and the body.

Draw the collar.

Draw in the buckle...

Cut stops on each side of the belt.

Trim back to it from the belt.

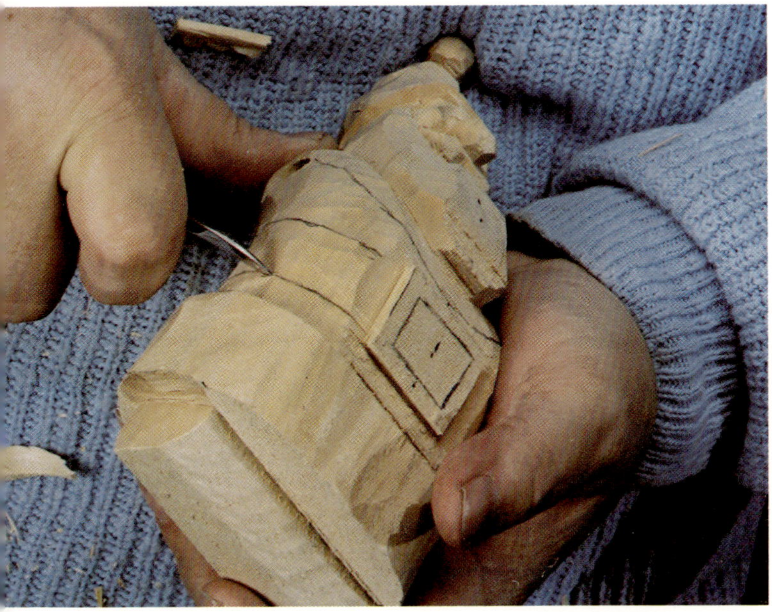

Cut stops around the top and bottom of the belt.

Cut back to the belt from the coat. I am cutting a pretty steep angle to give the appearance of the belt cutting into Santa's belly, to get that "bowl full of jelly" look.

Progress report.

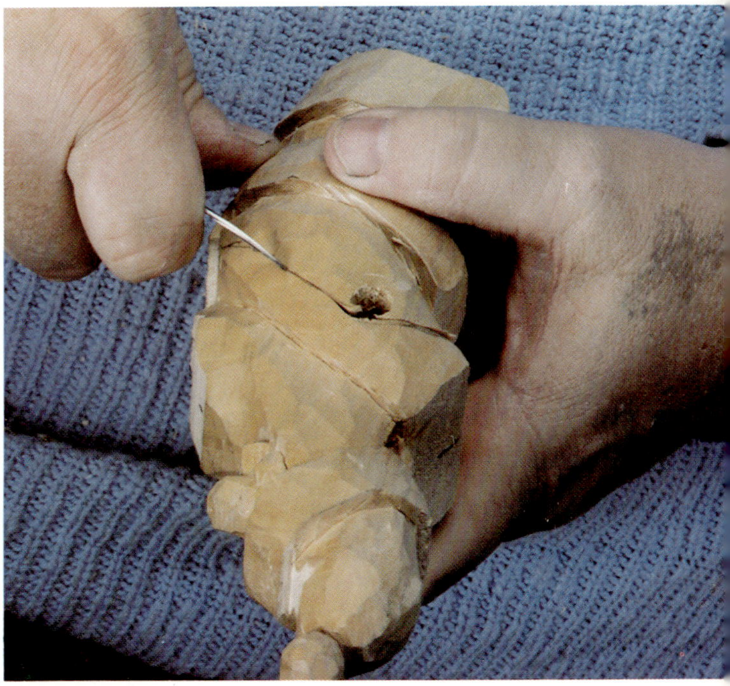

Cut a stop around the collar.

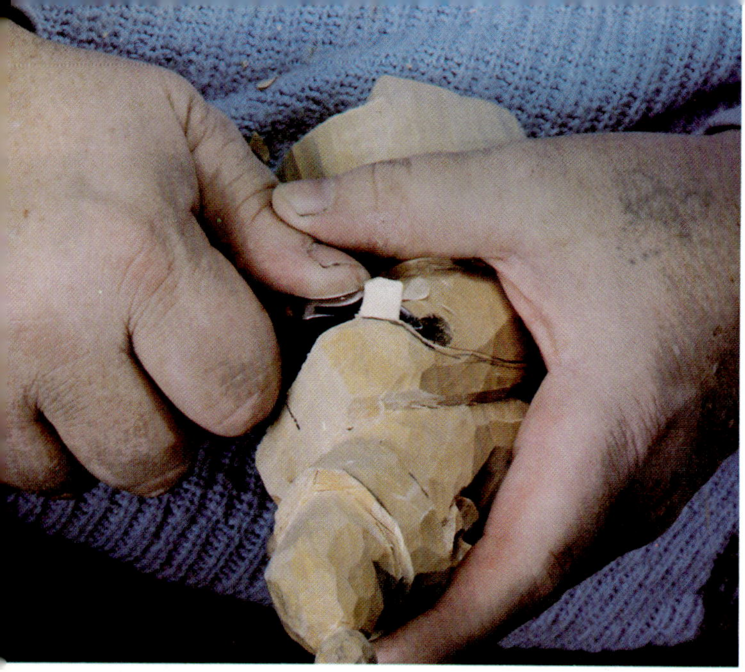

Trim back to it from the coat.

Go over the whole piece and clean up the rough spots, removing imperfections and saw marks like these on the back.

The finished collar.

Draw in the lines for the back of the beard, the hairline and the bottom of the ear.

Score the line at the back of the beard keeping the knife at an angle so it looks like it turns under.

Come back along that line and cut a slice.

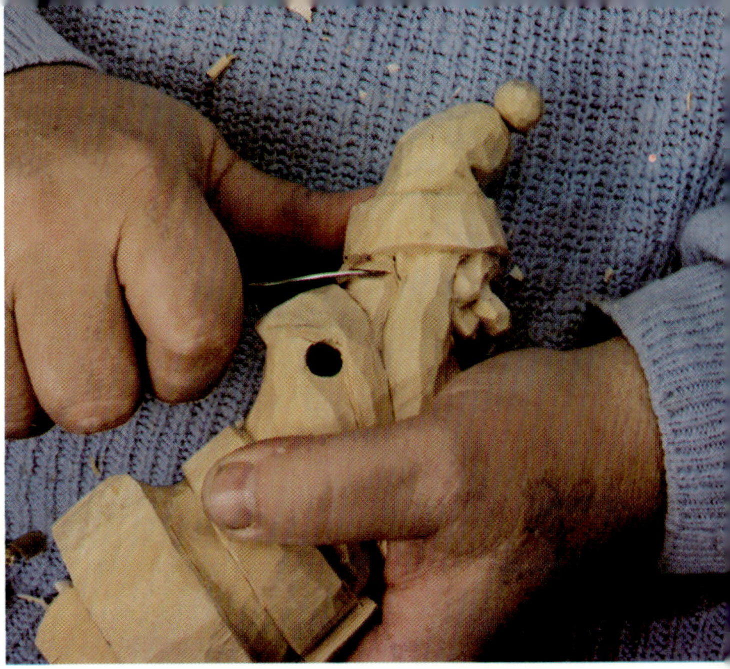

Make a stop along the hairline and cut back to it from the neck.

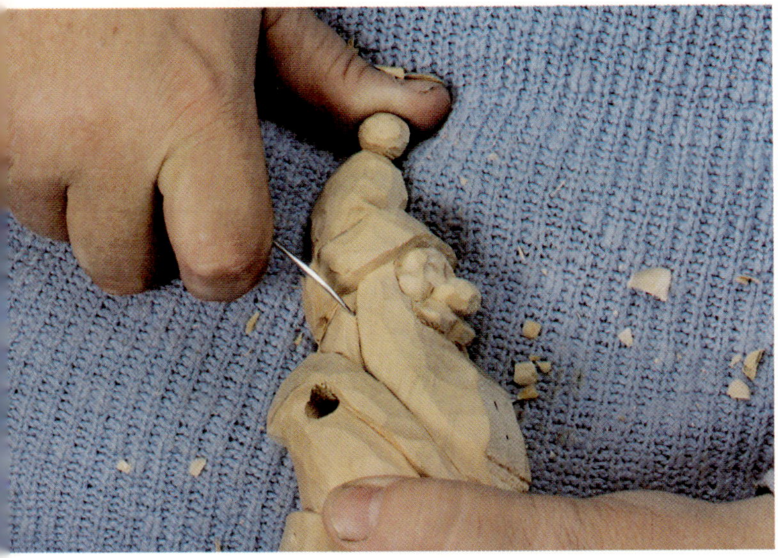

Remark the ear and cut a stop along the line.

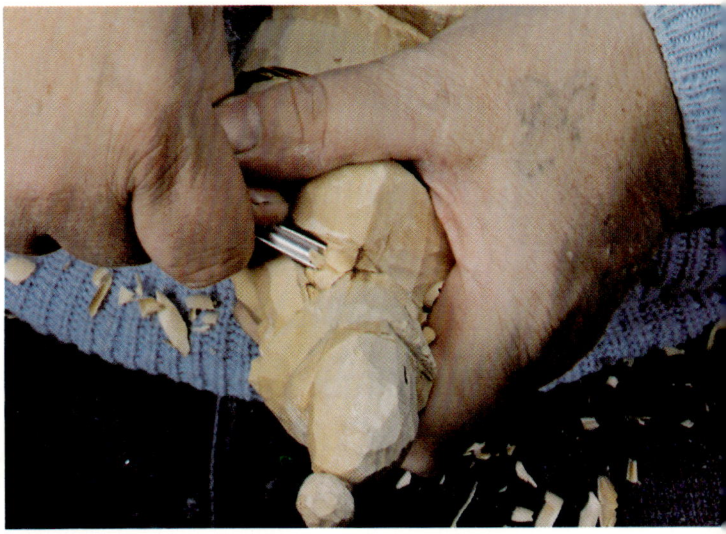

Remove the excess wood from the neck with a gouge.

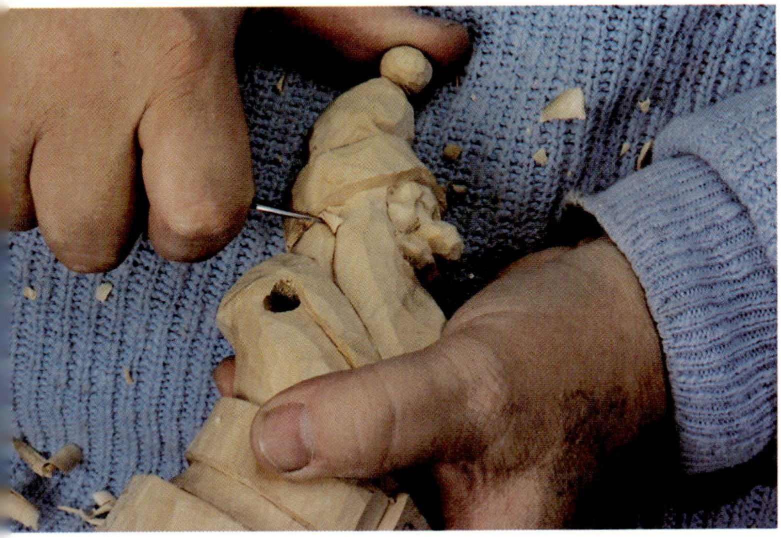

Trim back to it from the neck.

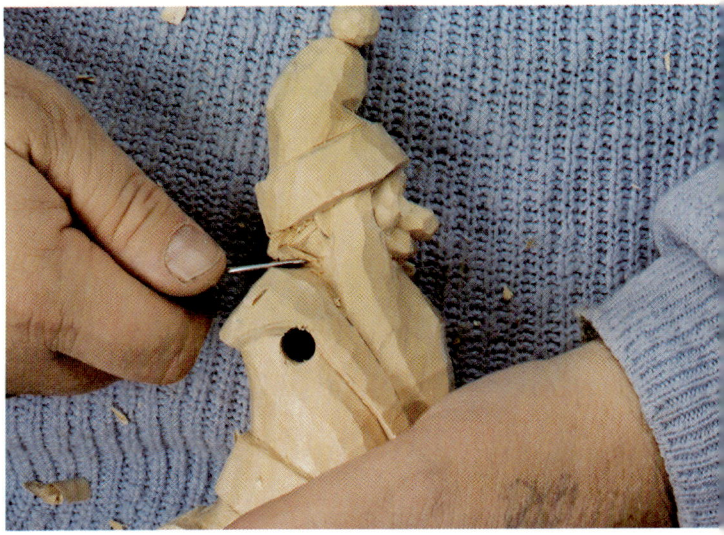

Clean up the neck and surrounding areas using a knife.

Mark the rump area, noting the areas to be removed.

Use a gouge to remove the unwanted wood.

You are looking for this result.

Cut the boots from stock. I use 4 inch stock, cut the pattern for the whole thickness, and then divide it four blanks, enough for two figures.

Draw the soles of the boots.

Pop off the sides to bring them down to the shape of the soles.

The roughly shaped boots.

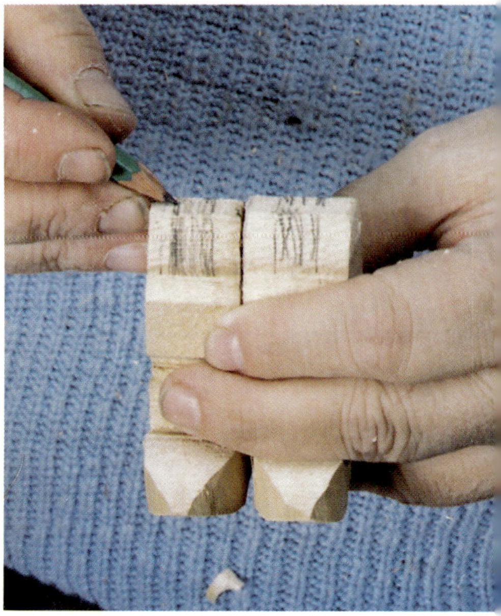

Using your finger as a gauge, mark the area to be removed at the top of the boot. This will make the joint with the leg. The exact measurement doesn't matter as long as it is thick enough to be strong on each edge.

Mark the cuff at the top of the boot.

Cut a stop at the bottom edge of the cuff...

and trim back to it from each of the four corners of the shoe.

When the corners are done continue around the cuff.

Trim the outside edges of the hinge by cutting a stop at the top of the boot and working back to it.

Returning to the boot, remove the corners to bring it down to an octagon shape.

After reaching the octagon, round the boot off, leaving some wood for a buckle.

Knock off the corners of the cuff.

Draw the buckle.

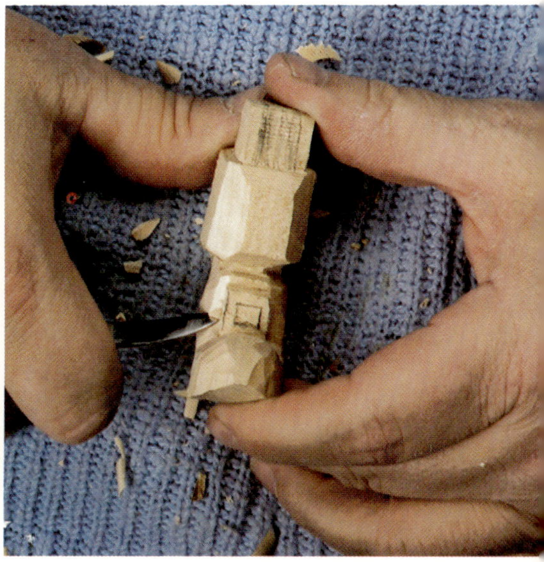

Cut a stop around the buckle and trim back to it.

Clean the boot and round the cuff.

Mark the instep of the boot and carve it away. This helps differentiate the left foot from the right foot.

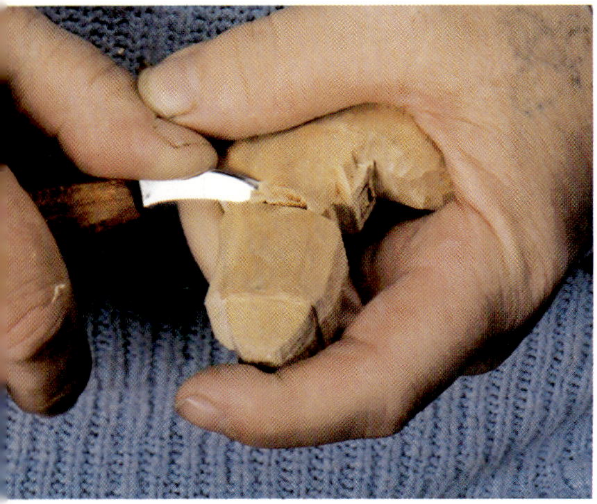

Look for uneven places, saw marks, sharp edges, and anything else that doesn't look right, and refine it.

To clean the inside of the buckle, begin by cutting a stop all the way around it.

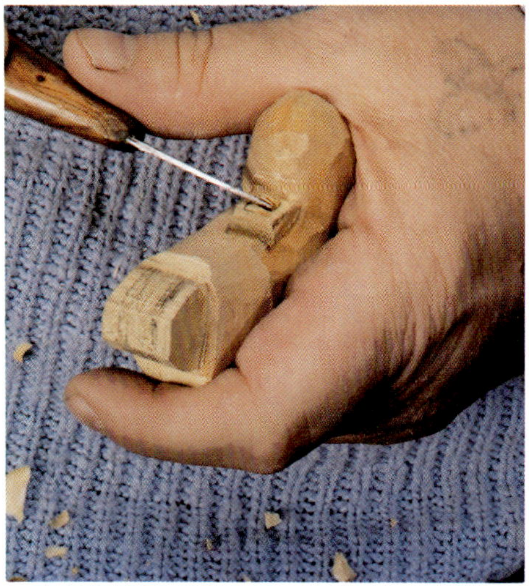

Using the point of your knife, cut back to the outside stops from the center of the buckle.

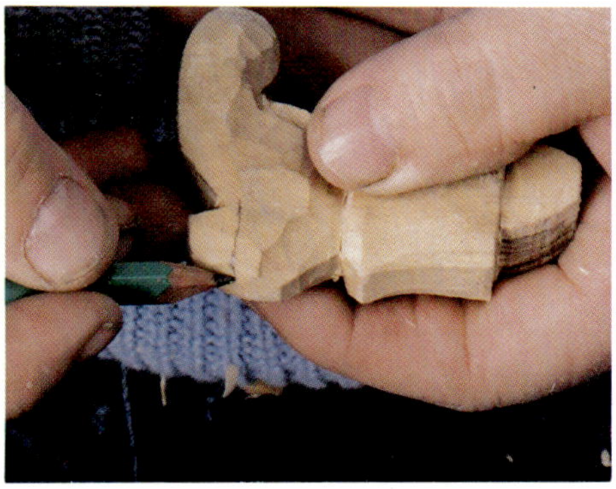

Draw the sole line. Begin at the heel, being sure that you start high enough to leave room for the sole. The tendency is to start right at the top of the heel instead of leaving that little bit extra.

Cut a stop all the way around the sole.

Cut back to the stop from the boot.

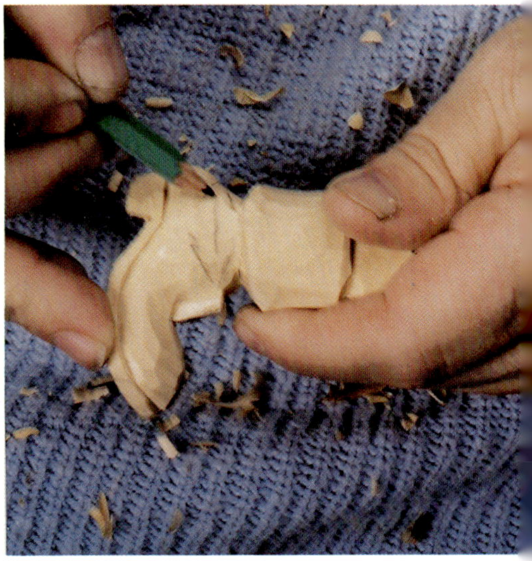

A natural looking fold in the boot is created with a pattern of cuts like this.

Cut the lines by slicing at a 45 degree angle along one side of the line, then along the other so the wedge pops out.

Clean the hinge with the knife.

Use a gouge to pop out the central area of the hinge. I make the boot portion of the hinge first and fit the thigh portion of the leg to it. This is much easier than trying to do exact measurements, which hardly ever turn out to be exact when hand carving.

Mark a spot in the center of the hinge where you will drill the hole for the pin.

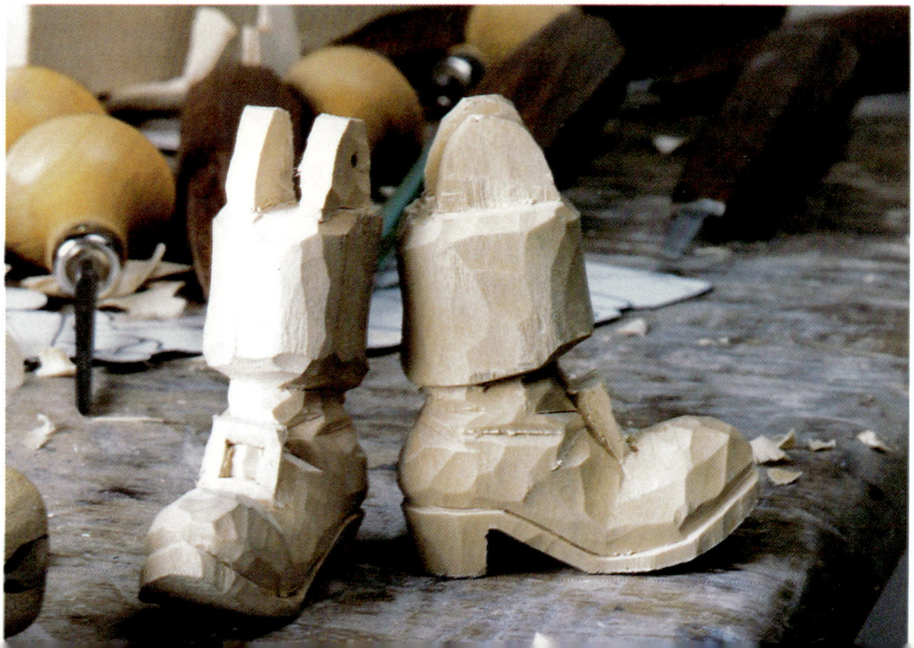

The finished boots.

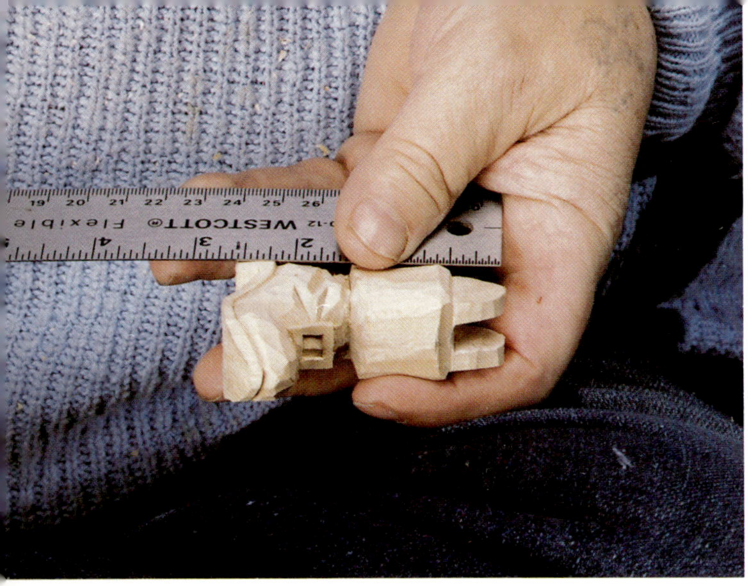

Measure the boot...

Cut the stock to length.

and transfer the length to the stock you will be using for the thigh.

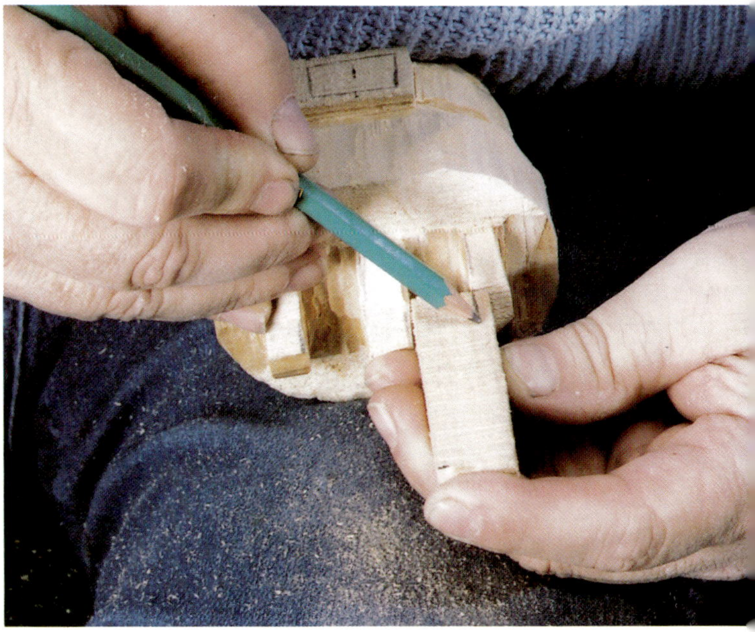

Mark the top of the thigh to fit in the hip hinge. First mark the width. I'm going to take it all from the outside of the thigh, which will give me more separation in the legs.

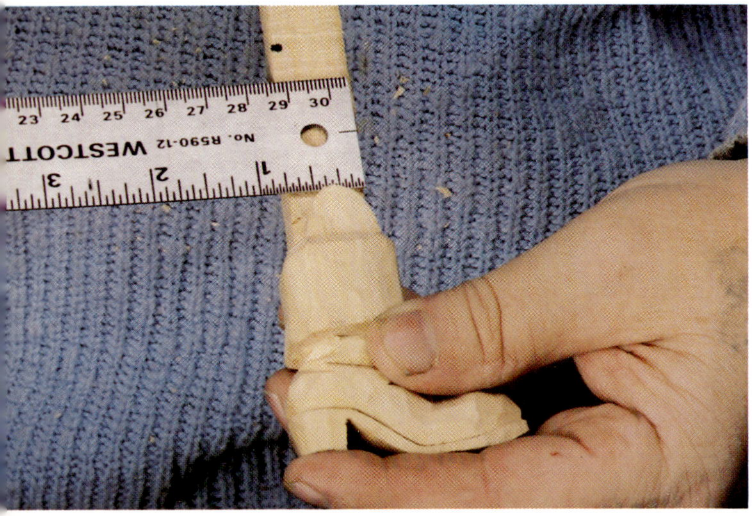

The thickness of the thigh should be about the same as the hinge.

Mark the depth of the hinge.

Number the hinge and the thigh. Each joint is custom fitted and will need to be numbered so you can put it back where it goes.

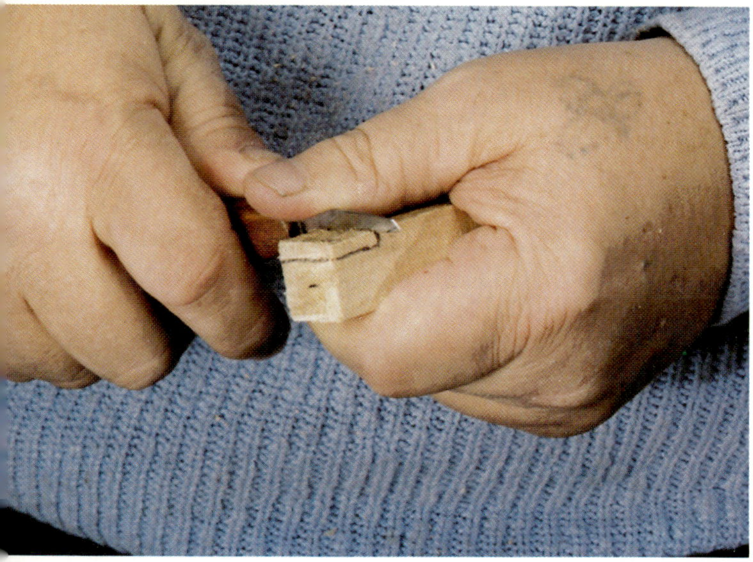

Cut a stop in the depth mark...

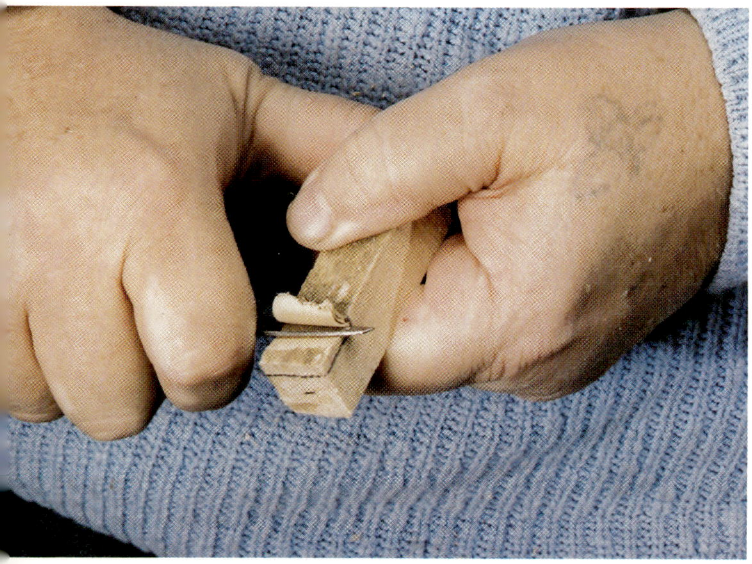

and remove the excess by cutting back to it.

The fit should be pretty snug. This helps in the drilling and placement of dowels, and will work loose as the figure is used.

Match a drill bit to the dowel you will use in the hinge. It should be a snug fit, even if you have to sand the dowel a little for it to fit.

Mark the center of the hip joint.

A little trick I use is to run my drill backward to mark the spot.

Then, with the leg in place, I drill from the outside of the hip, through the leg, and into the middle hip. I don't go all the way through the middle piece.

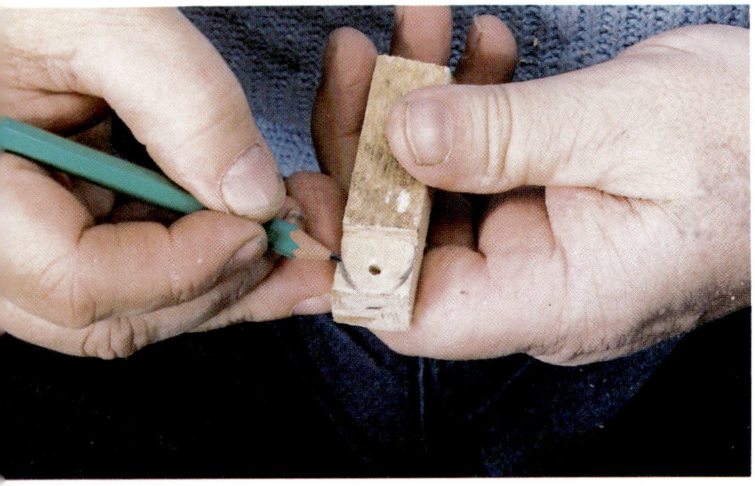

Mark the end of the leg where you will round it, allowing it to swing in the joint.

Shape the end with the knife.

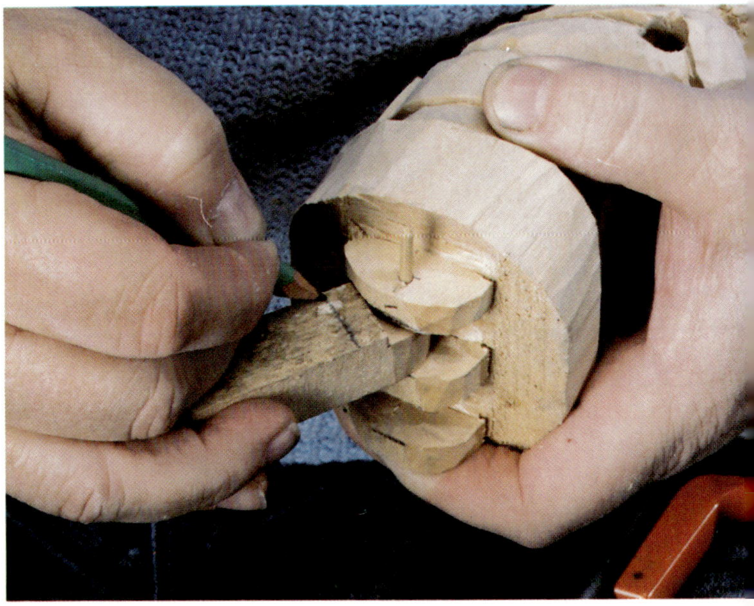

A test fitting shows me that the leg is not swinging as far as I want. I can either trim the leg or the hip to fix this. I want to keep the hip large, so I'll trim the leg to this mark.

This gives me the swing I want. No matter what pattern you use, these adjustments will have to be made for a good fit. Do the other leg in the same way. Remember to number the joint on the hip and the leg.

When drilling the hole for the second dowel I like to eyeball it to get as straight a line as possible. Functionally this is not crucial because we use two separate dowels, but aesthetically it helps the appearance of the Santa.

Again, you will always have to tune things up a bit. This time the hip joint was pinching the second leg and had to be cleaned up.

With the left leg and the left foot, mark the width...

and the depth of the hinge tenon.

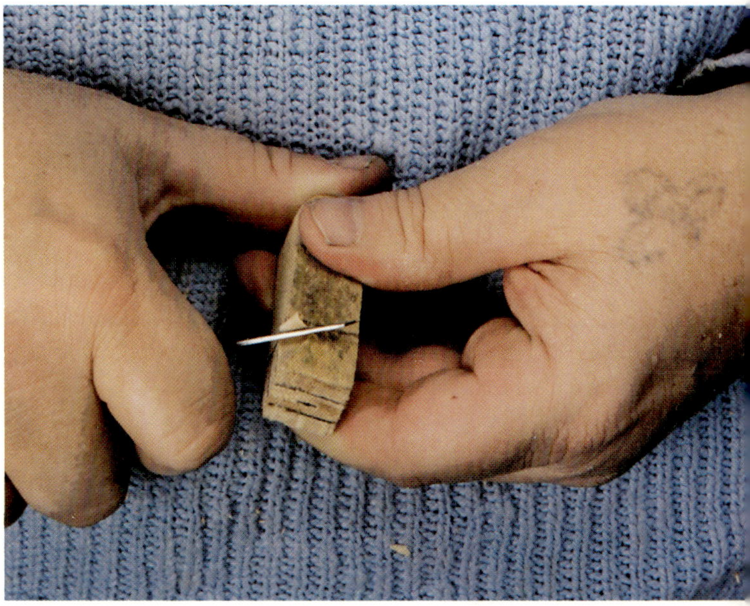

Begin at the corners and use the stop and slice technique to remove the sides of the tenon.

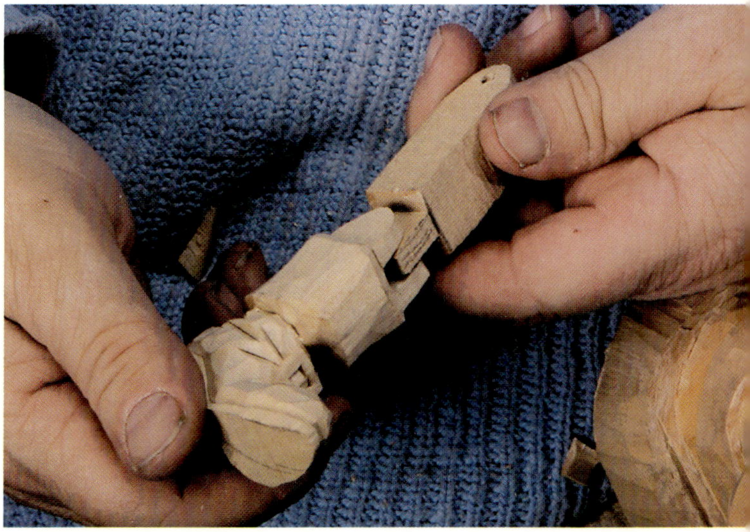

Fit the leg to the boot and make any adjustments necessary.

To make a knee joint you only round the back side of the tenon. This keeps the leg from pivoting too far forward.

Mark the center for the pivot pin and drill the hole for the pin. Remember to have the pieces together when you drill.

After you drill, cut away the area you marked in the knee joint. You will probably have to fine tune everything to make it work the way you want. By moving the joint, the rubbing creates shiny places where there is too much wood. This is a good way of knowing where you need to trim.

A test fitting of the left leg.

Moving to the arms now, run the dowel through the body and mark it, leaving enough at each end for the width of the arm.

Remove the dowel and mark the width of the arm at each end.

To create a tenon on each end of the shoulder dowel, cut a stop on the mark you have just made...

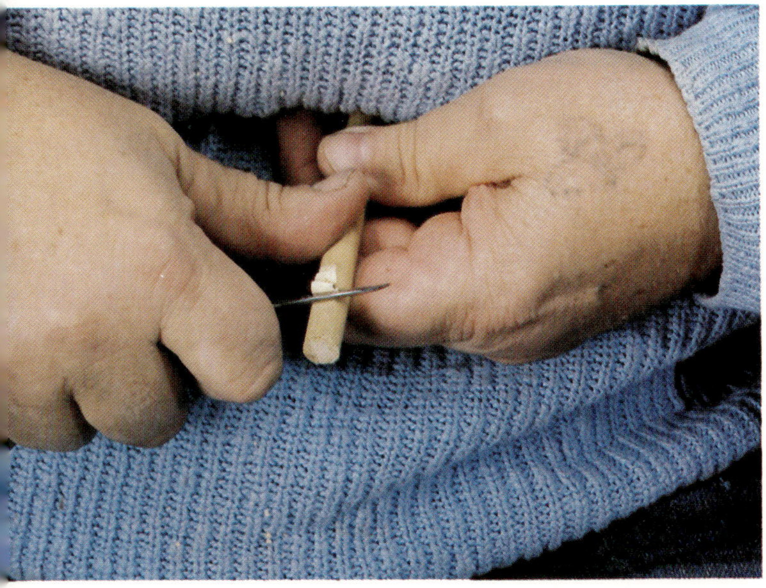

and cut back to it.

When you have finished one surface of the tenon, mark the other surface to be parallel and carve it down. You want to keep this tenon fairly thick for strength.

When one end is completed, carry the lines to the other end of the dowel, using your finger as a depth guide. Repeat the carving at that end.

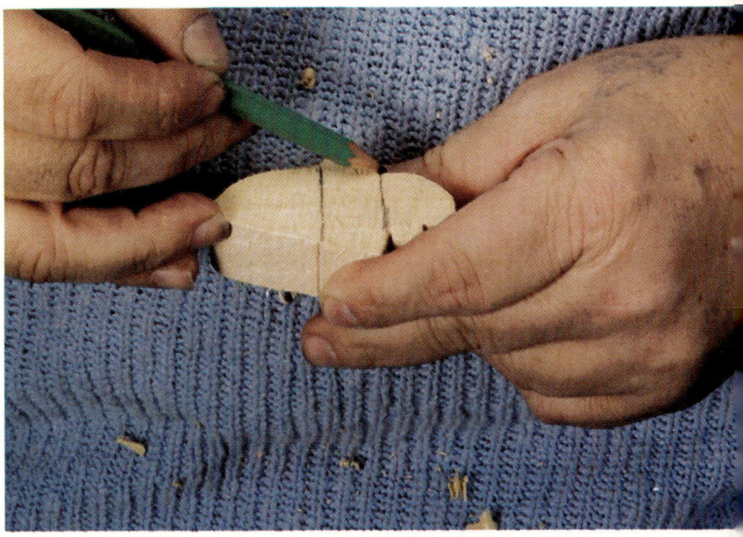

Move to the mitten blank. Like the boot blank, this was cut from 4 inch stock, and then sliced to produce four blanks. Mark the cuff.

Use the stop and trim method on the forearms above the cuff. Remember begin on the corners.

Do the same at the glove.

Remove the area with a gouge. This is most easily done if you work in from either side toward the middle. Again, use the forefinger of the knife hand as a depth gauge/ safety stop. Use a knife to clean up the cut.

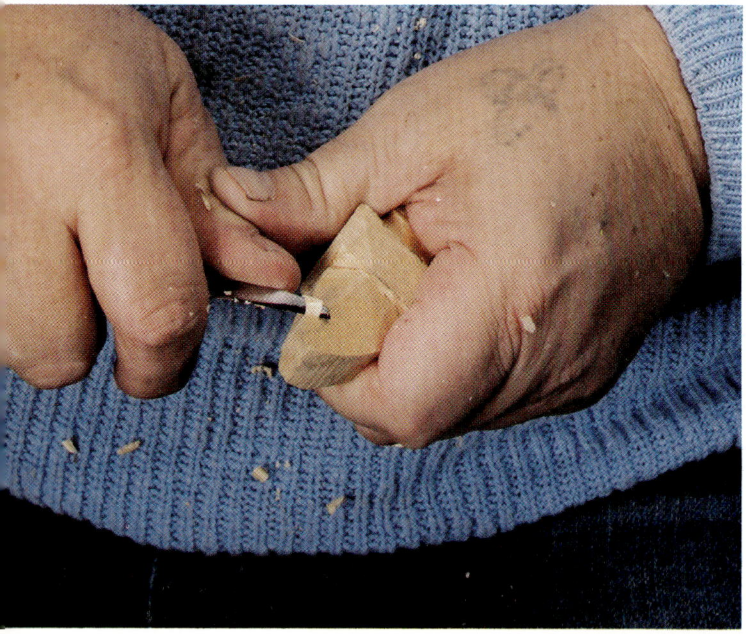

Back at the forearms, after narrowing them a bit, leave the surfaces fairly flat and knock off the corners up to the elbow.

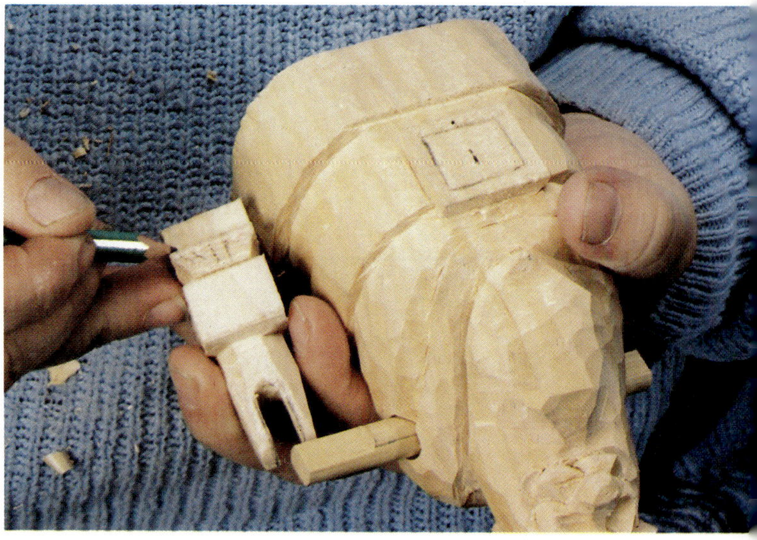

Hold the hand next to the piece and mark the thumb (next to the body) and the area to be removed.

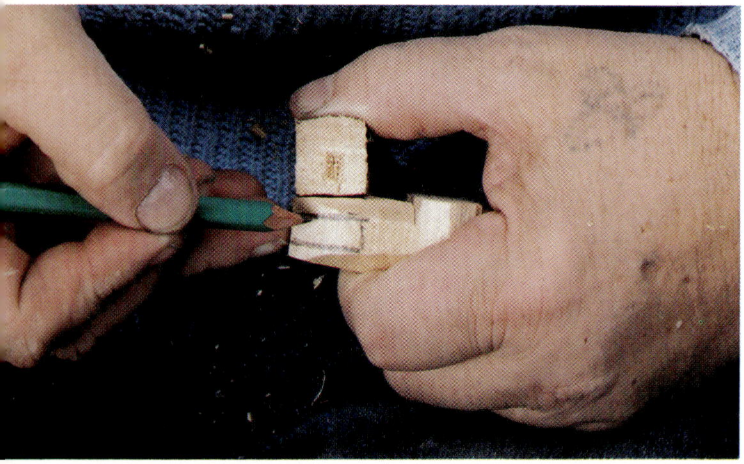

Mark the mortise of the elbow joint, using the upper arm stock as a guide to depth.

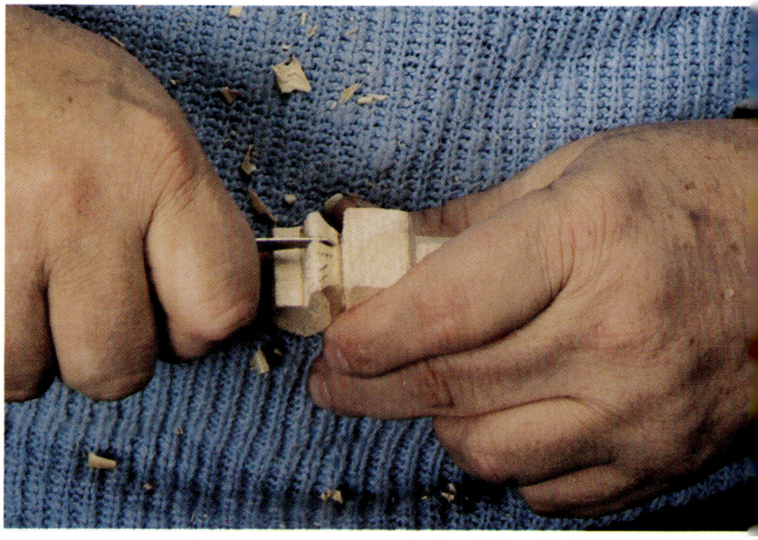

Make a stop in the thumb line...

and cut back to it across the palm of the mitten.

On the inside of the hand, again mark the thumb and the area to be removed in front of it.

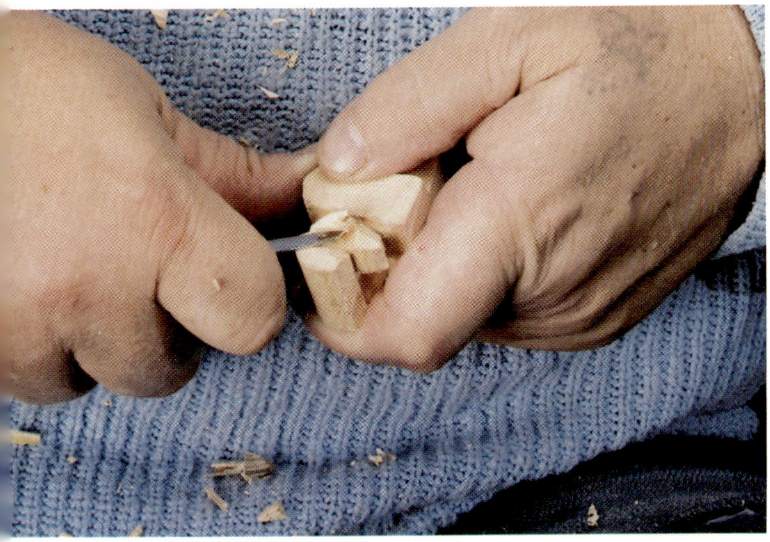

Cut a stop in the thumb line and remove the marked area.

Mark the area to be removed on the backside of the hand, making it thinner.

Remove the excess for this result.

Knock the corners off the cuff, and carve and refine it until it is nicely rounded. Repeat the process on the other hand, but be careful! It's easy to get turned around and end up with two left hands! Check and double check.

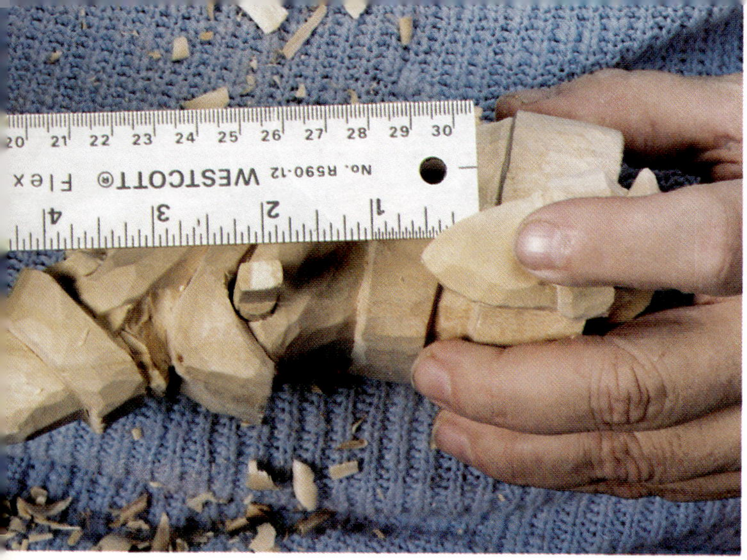

I want the hands to hang a little bit below the coat. To determine the length of the upper arm, I hold the forearms in place and measure from the bottom of the mortise to the top of the shoulder dowel. In this case it comes to about 2¼ inches. Mark the arm stock and cut off two pieces of that length.

Hold the upper arm to the shoulder and mark the width...

and depth of the mortise you need. Remember each joint is unique, so measure them individually and mark them for future matching.

As with the leg, clean out the mortise by carving from both sides to the middle using a gouge. Fine tune the carving with a knife.

With the upper arm held in place mark the areas of the arm and shoulder dowel that need to be removed to give the arm the proper look. Trim both down to size.

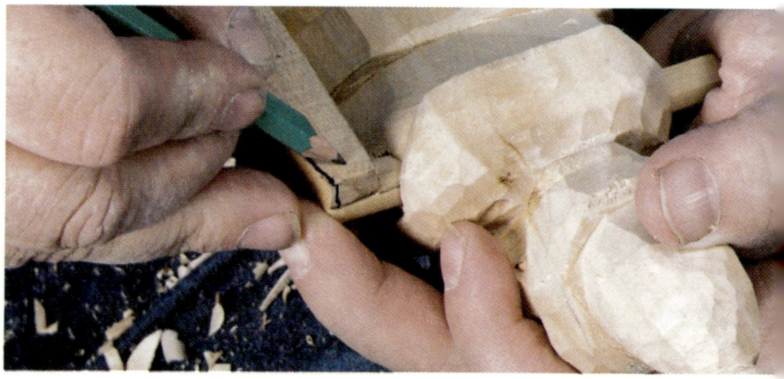

Mark the center pivot point of the upper arm while holding it in place.

Because it is hard to hold it in place while drilling I remove the arm to drill the hole through the first portion of the joint.

I then put arm in place and drill it enough to mark the spot in the shoulder dowel. I finish the hole in the shoulder dowel after I take the arm off.

Then I put the drill back in the arm and complete the hole through the other side of the arm joint.

To get the pivot I want I am going to have to round the inside of the top of the arm...

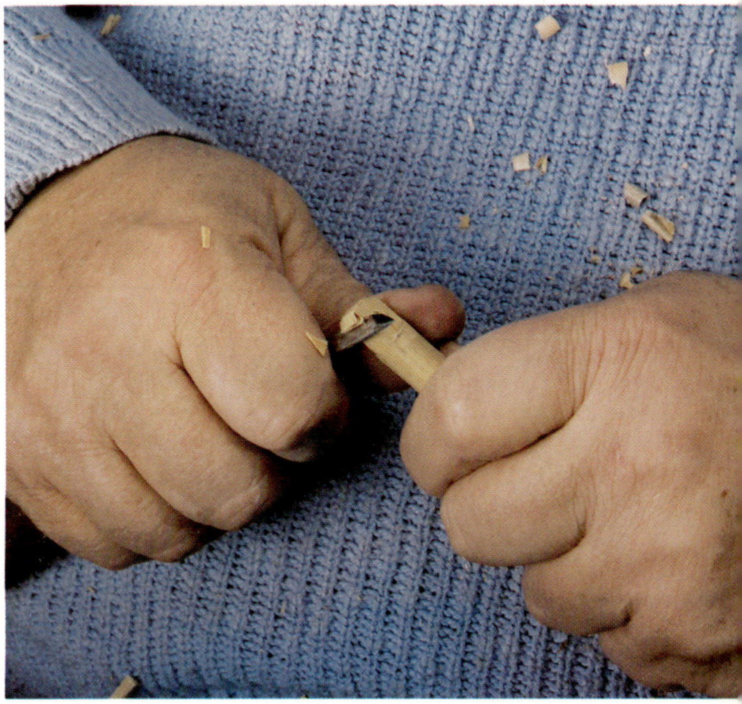

and the end of the dowel. Continue the adjustment until the arm moves freely.

Still not satisfied with the movement, I round off the outside of the top of the upper arm.

The tenon at the elbow joint runs diagonally. This lets the arm make a more natural movement toward the mouth instead of straight up and down. Use the stop and trim method to remove the waste beside the tenon.

Connect the mitten to the upper arm, mark the hole and drill a hole for the dowel. Round the ends of the tenon so that the joint will move easily.

A trial fitting before continuing is a good idea. Do the other arm to this point, following the same steps.

Here is Santa so far. All his joints seem in order. Now all we have to do is refine the limbs and the body and add some details.

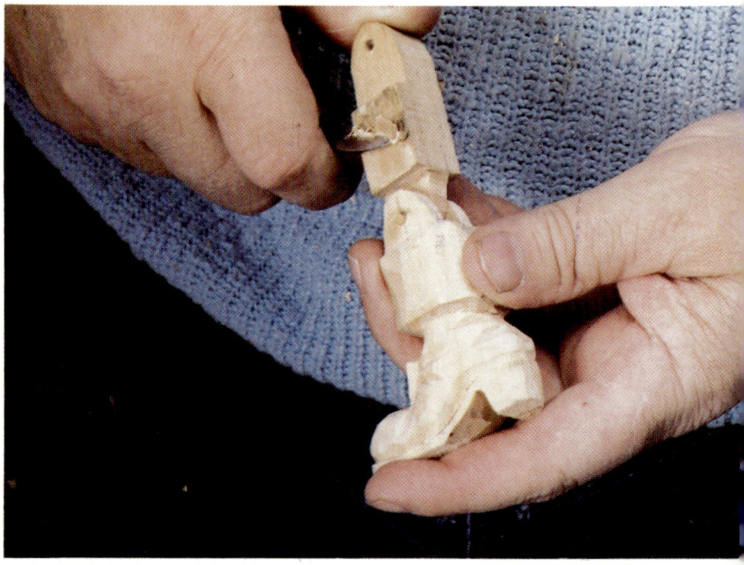

I usually take one leg or arm off at a time to avoid confusion. All I really have to do at this time is round things off, clean up rough places, and make minor adjustments.

The rounded legs and arms. Now we can disassemble things to work on the body.

Begin by finishing the details of the face. With a gouge start at the temples and cup out beside the eyes.

Round off the cheek with a knife.

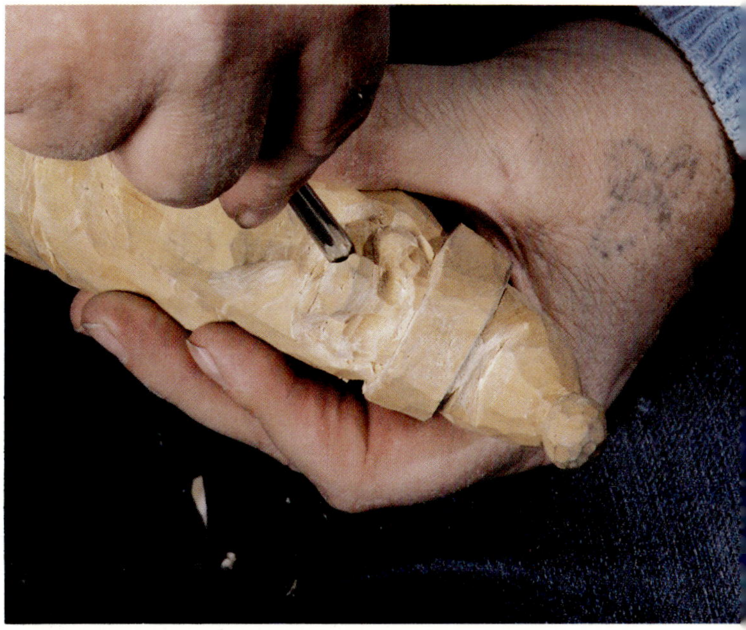

Using a half-round gouge with the cup away from the nose, push in at the nostril. Go straight in and stop without prying.

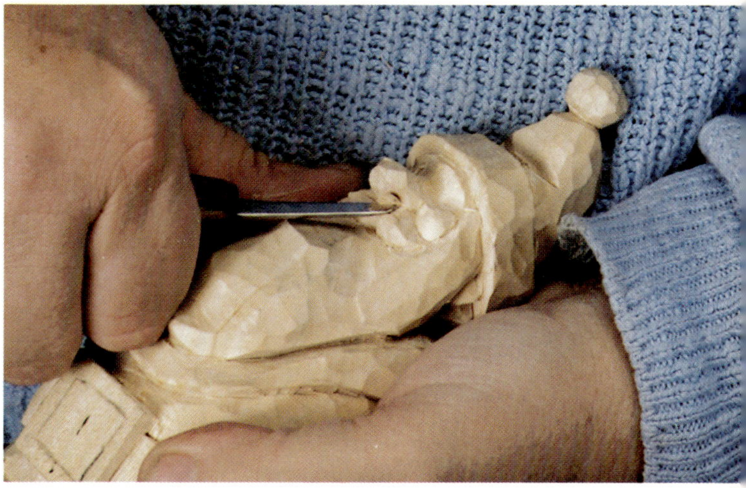

Cut off the piece with a knife.

With the same gouge, start at the front of the nose and go over the flair of the nostril.

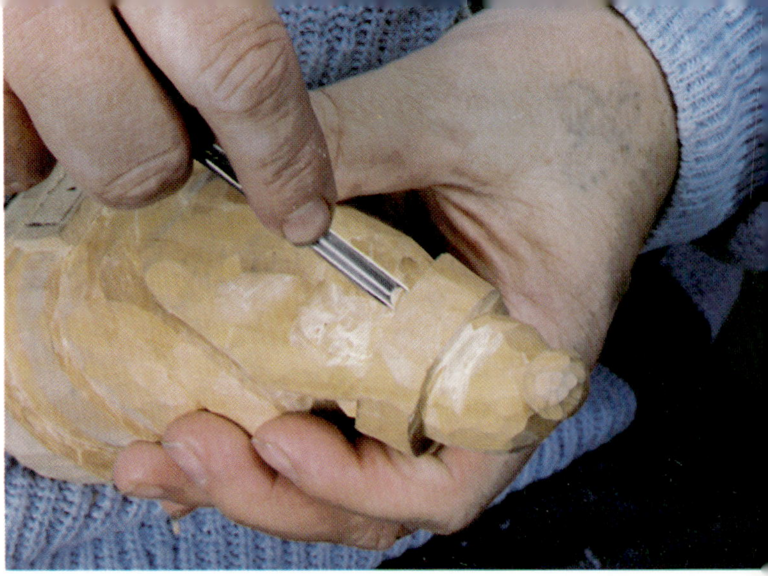

Make a nitch between the eyebrows.

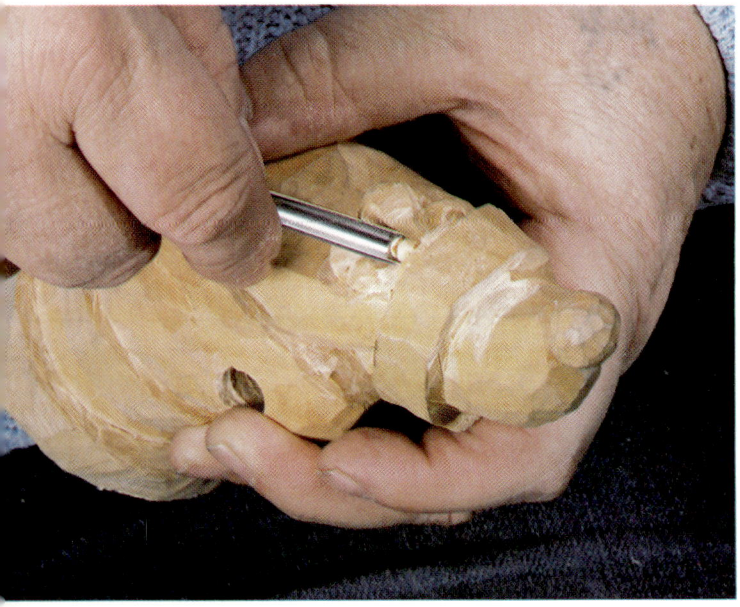

Continue up into the eye socket.

Clean out the eye socket.

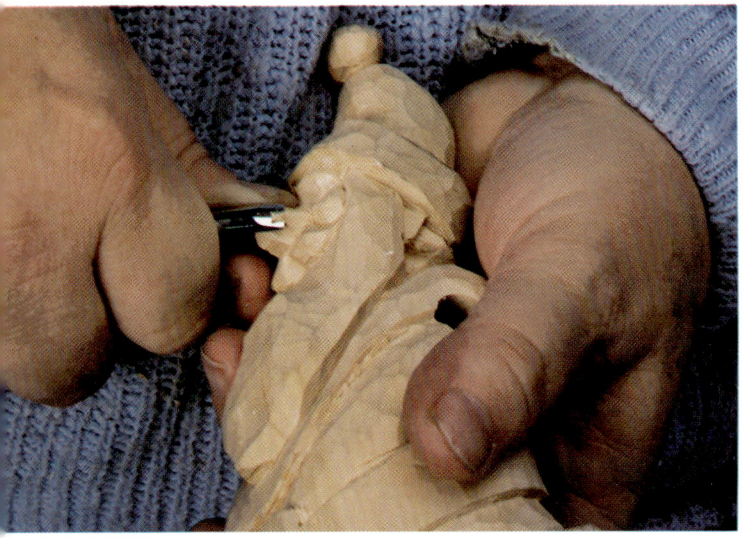

Go back with the gouge and scoop out a little at the front of the nostril.

With the cup side up, push into the top edge of the moustache, giving it a little more of a curled look.

Come across the jaw with a gouge, creating the insinuation of a bottom lip.

Create the corners of the eyes by first carving straight in along the line of the upper lid.

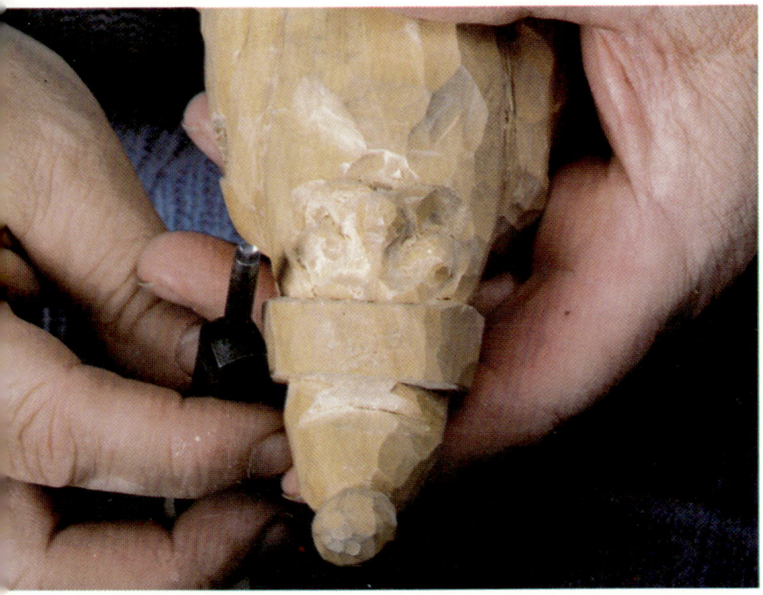

Hold the eyepunch next to the face to be sure the size is right for the eyes.

Then cut the bottom lid line in the same way.

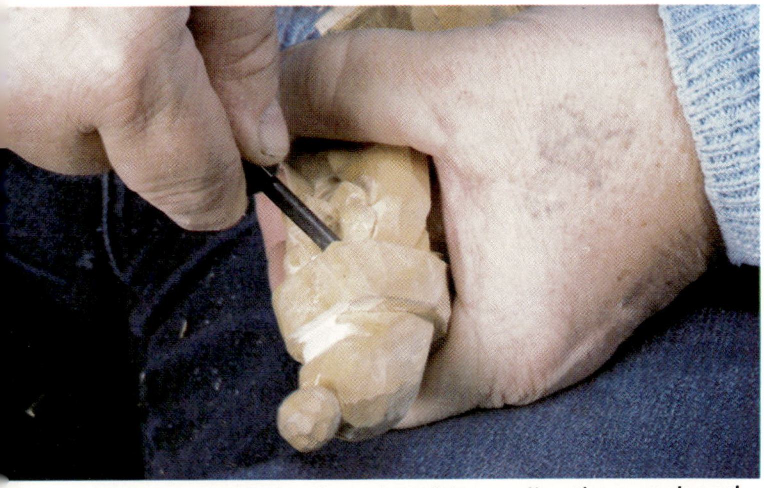

Beginning with the figure's right eye, align the punch and push and twist. Do the left eye next. This makes it easier to make sure the eyes are aligned.

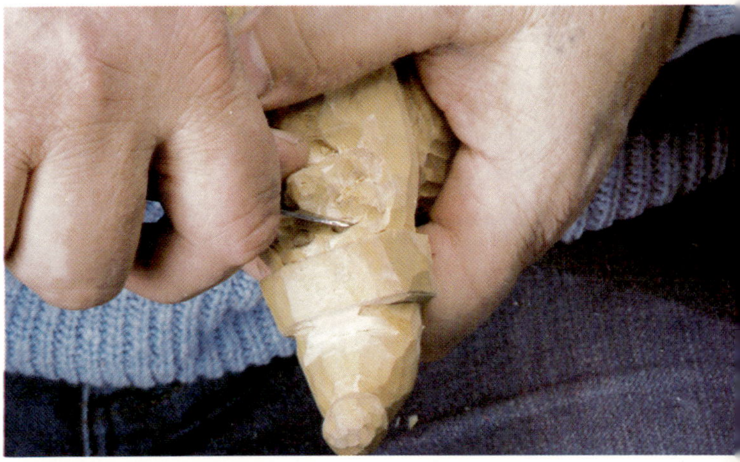

Finally situate your blade so that it is flat along the curve of the eyeball and push it into the corner to pop out the triangular wedge. If it needs it, repeat the process on the inside corners of the eyes.

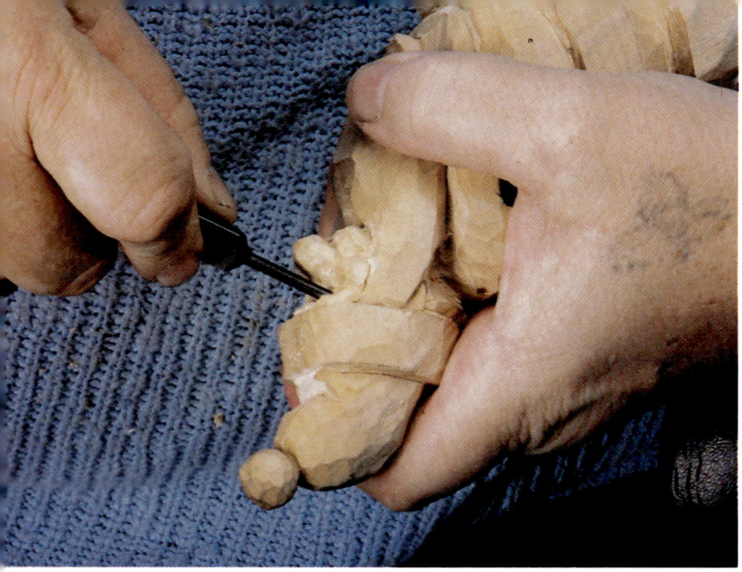

With a smaller eyepunch, push and turn to form the pupil. It works best to have the figure looking up a bit.

Clean and do a final shaping of the body. I leave a lot of chips in this piece to give it a folksy look.

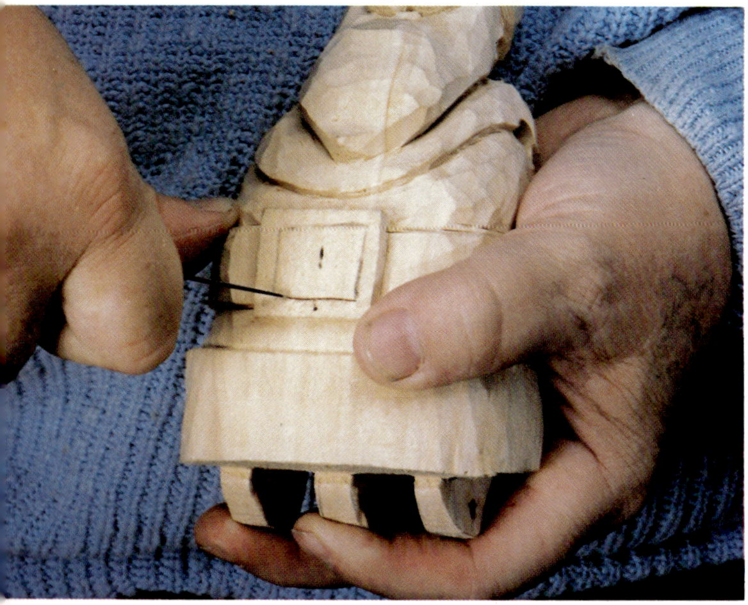

Cut a stop all around the inside of the belt buckle.

Slice back to the stop all around.

The body is ready for painting.

Painting the Jointed Santa

I use Winsor and Newton Alkyd tube paints for nearly all my painted carvings. These are thinned with pure turpentine to a consistency that is soaked into the carving, giving subtle colors. What I look for is a watery mixture, almost like a wash. In this way the turpentine will carry the pigment into the wood, giving the stained look I like. It has always been my theory that if you are going to cover the wood, why use wood in the first place. It should be noted that with white, the concentration of the pigment should be a little stronger.

I mix my paints in juice bottles, putting in a bit of paint and adding turpentine. I don't use exact measurements. Instead I use trial and error, adding a bit of paint or a bit of turpentine until I get the thickness I want.

The juice bottles are handy for holding your paints. They are reclosable, easy to shake, and have the added advantage of leaving a concentrated amount of color on the inside of the lid and the sides of the bottle which can be used when more intense color is needed.

Begin with the face. Start with a mixture of tube flesh, raw sienna, and white. Cover the face area, ears, neck, and lips.

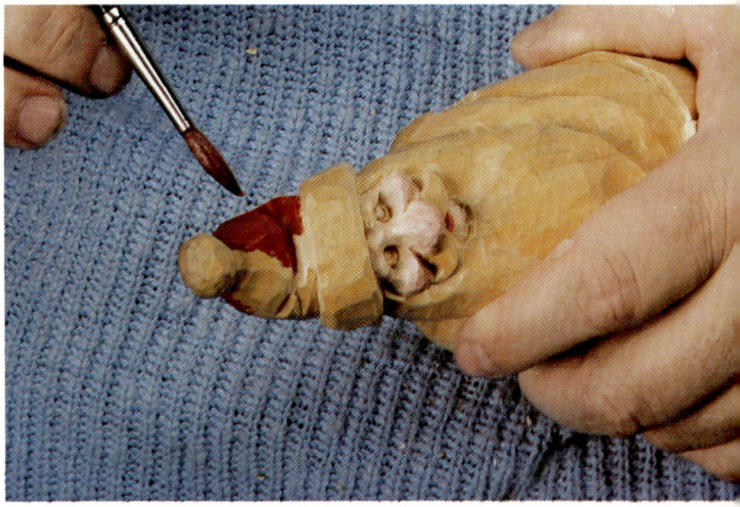

Apply alizarin red to the cap.

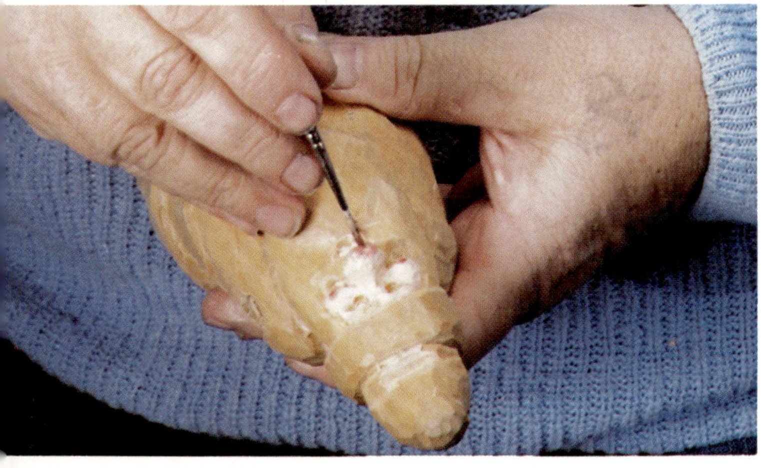

Put touches of red paint on the cheeks, nose, lips and ears. Blend it in with the brush.

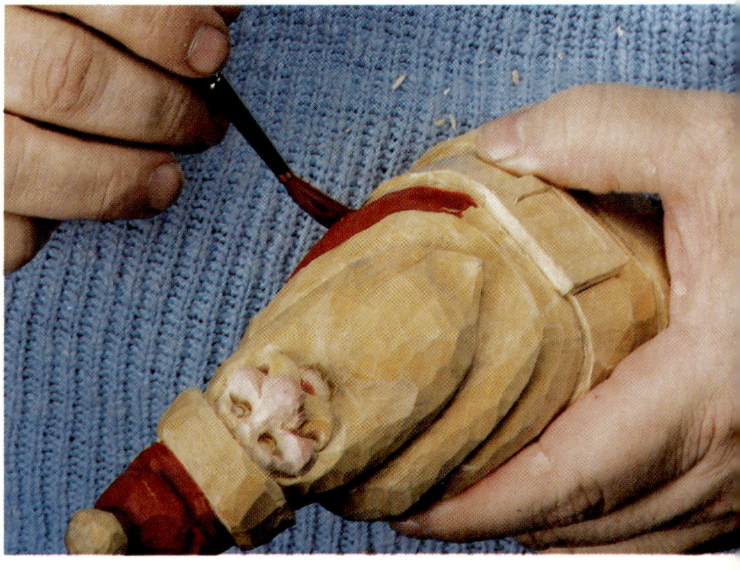

Continue the red on the coat.

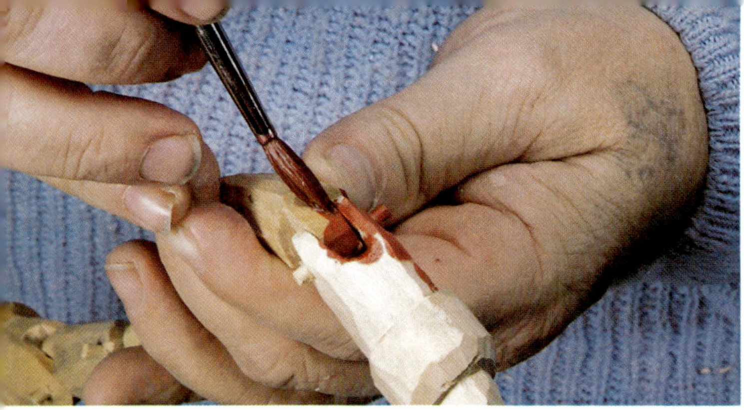

Paint the arm assembly red, soaking the paint into the joints. I only paint the shoulder dowel as far as it can be seen. Don't paint the cuffs or mittens yet.

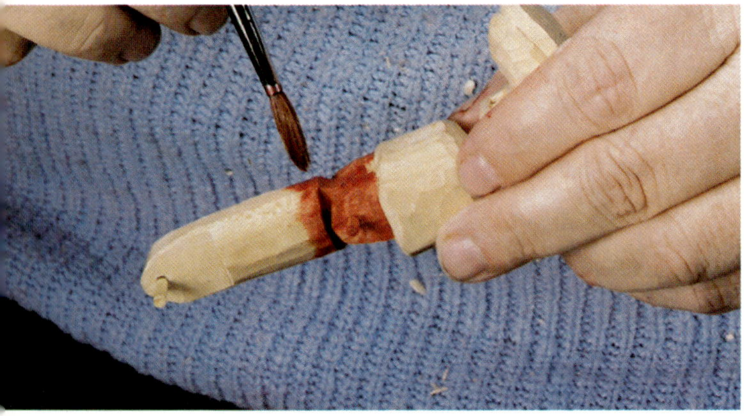

Do the top of the leg in red.

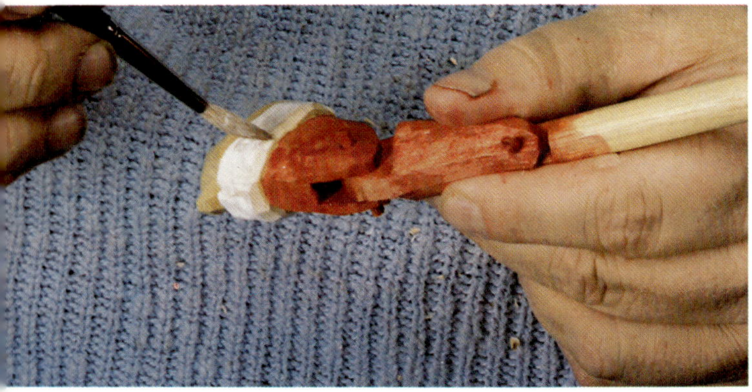

Shift to white and begin with the cuffs of the sleeves.

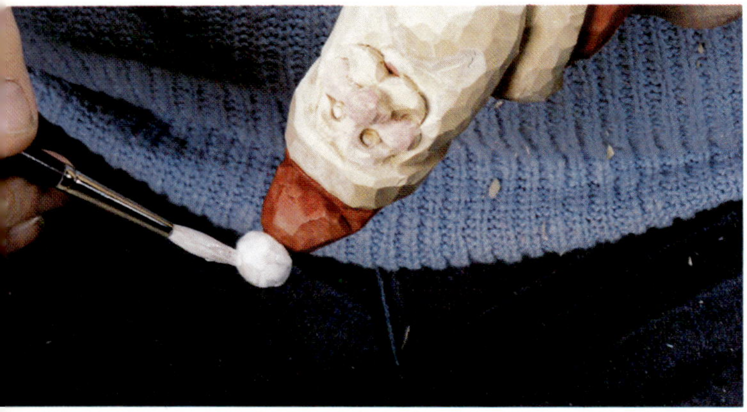

White goes on the ball of the cap...

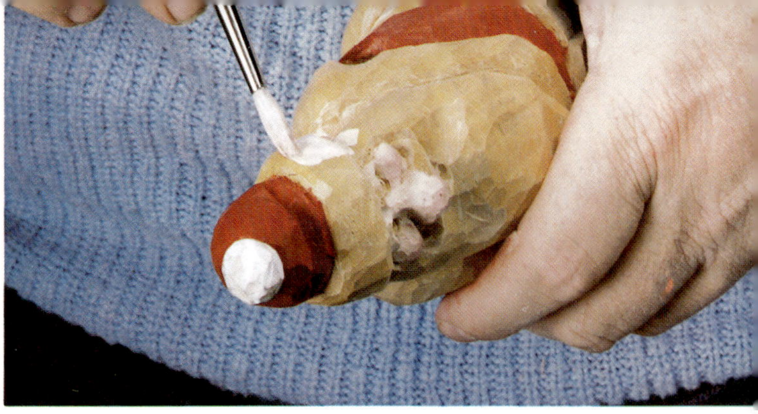

its fur trim...

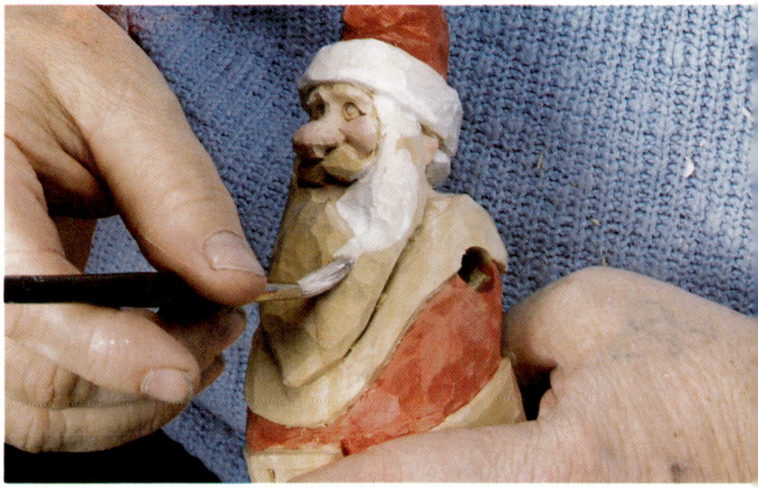

beard and moustache...

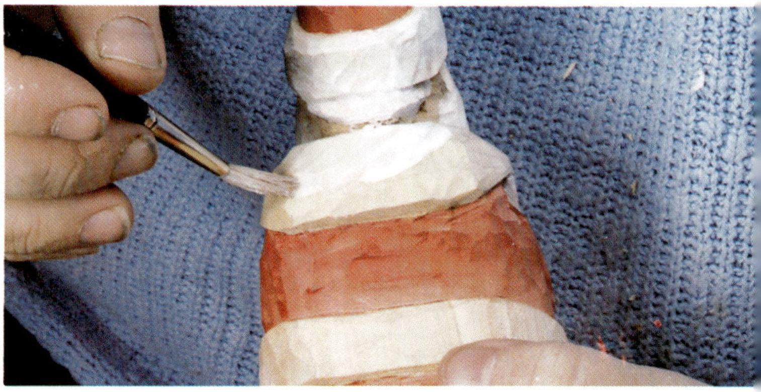

collar...

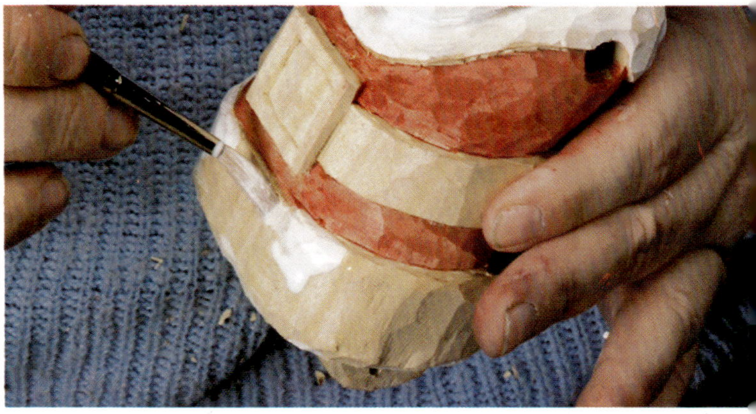

and the fur of the coat.

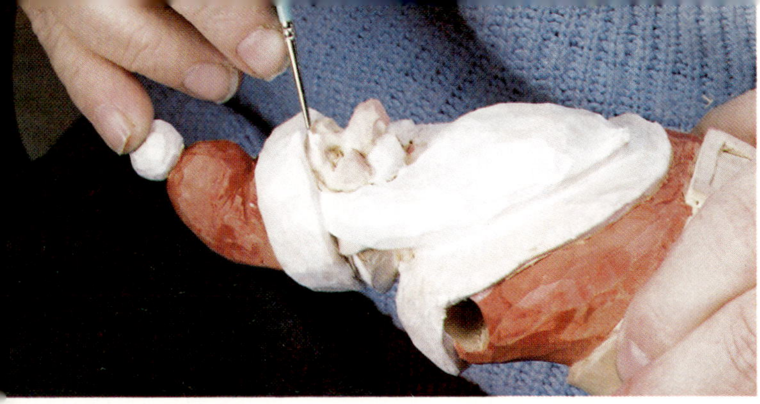

With a smaller brush paint the eyebrows. For this I pour most of the paint back in the bottle, leaving only a residue in the cap. This is richer in pigment and covers well.

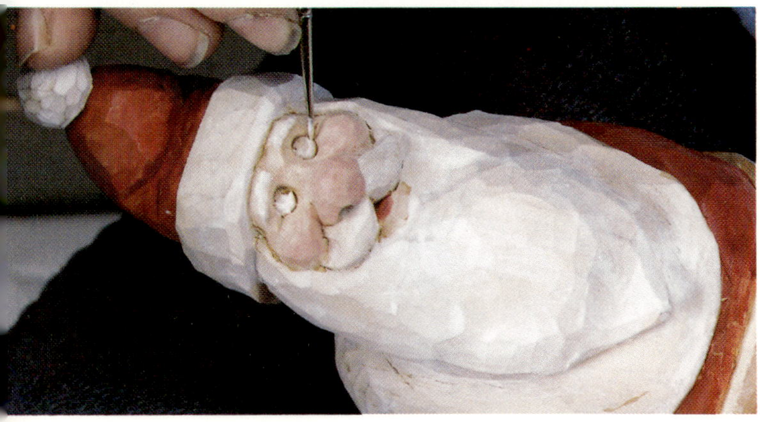

Use this same white for the eyes. It's alright to paint the whole eye and come back and cover it with blue.

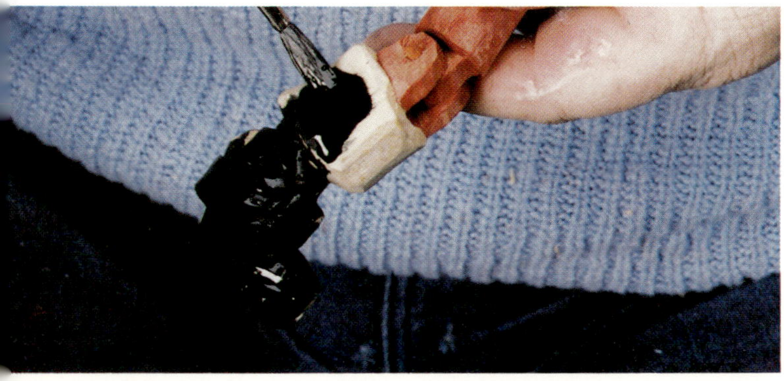

Switch to black paint and cover the boots...

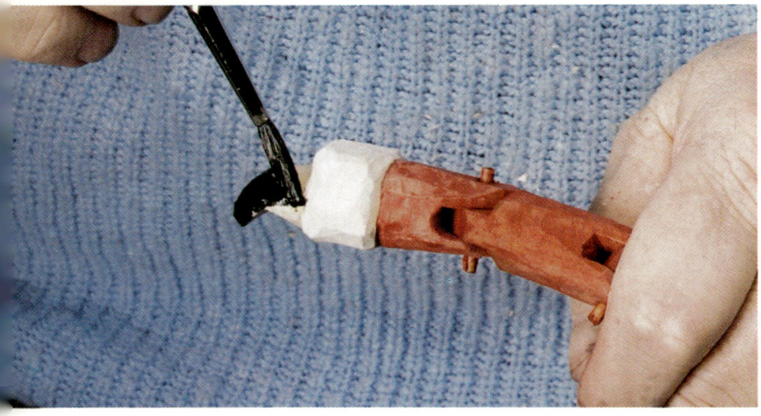

the mittens...

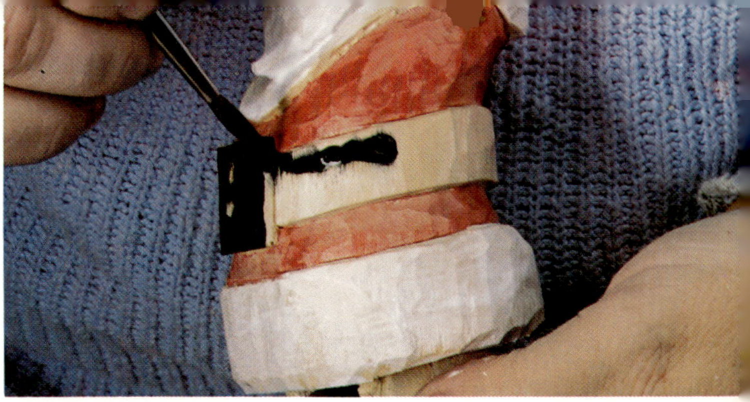

and the belt.

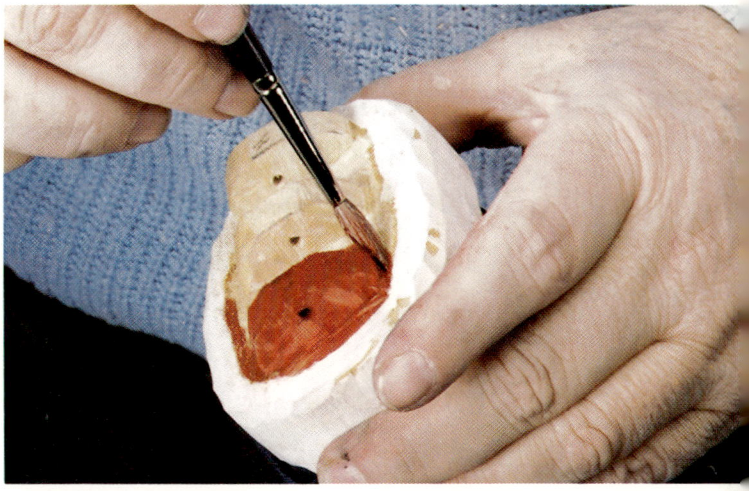

Now that I don't need it to hold the figure, I can paint the area of the hip hinge with alizarin red.

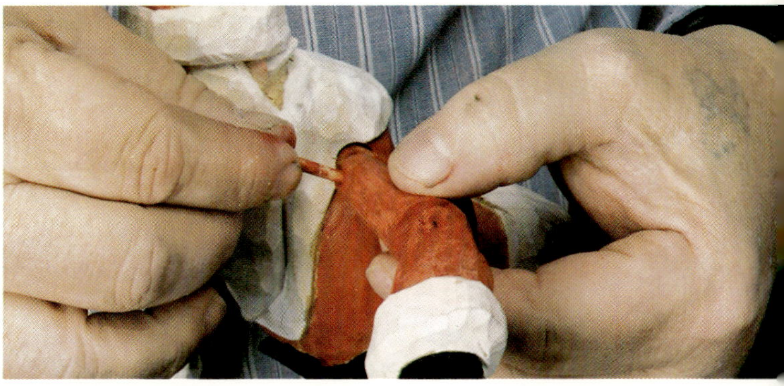

Assemble Santa.

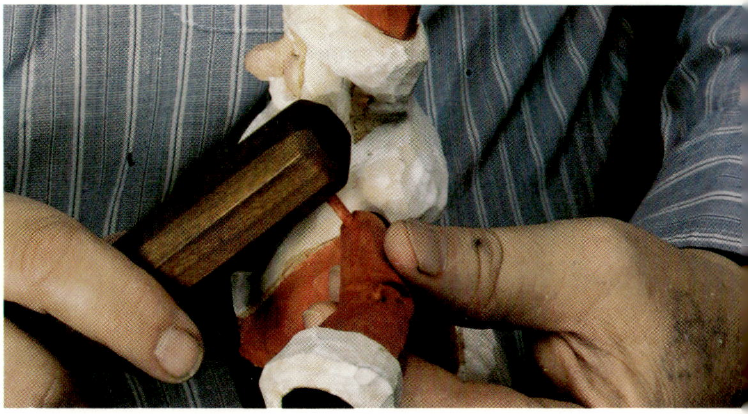

Tap the pegs in place.

I clip off the ends of the pegs with a bonsai snipper. It is a great tool for cutting small diameter things right down to flush. You should be able to find one in a catalog or from a dealer in bonsai supplies. If you can't find one, you can make this cut with a knife.

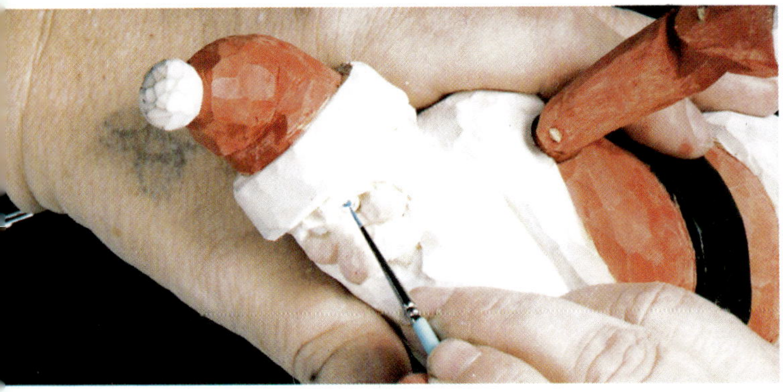

Now to finish up the painting, we will add blue to the eyes. I use my thumb as a pallet and a very fine brush. I take the paint from the jar cap where the pigments are concentrated. The mark from the smaller eyepunch defines the area for painting and helps keep the paint in place.

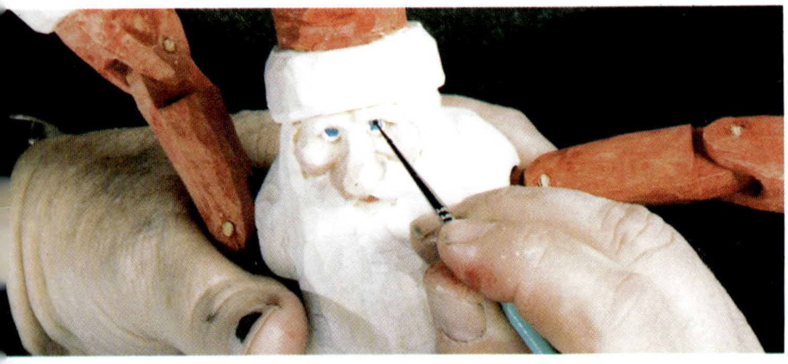

In the same way, use black to add a pupil to the eye.

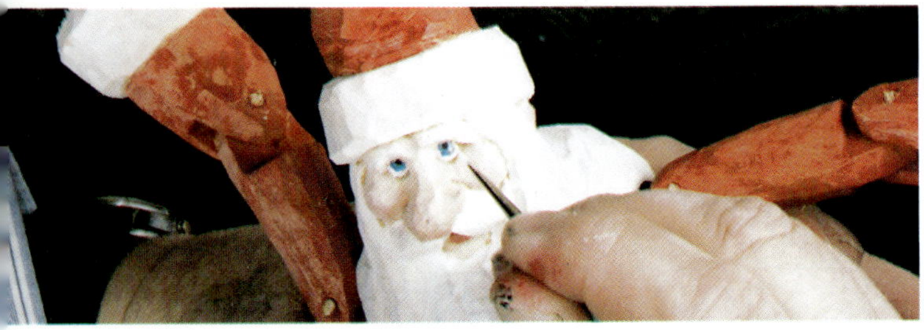

Finally add a "ee-nigh tiny" white dot for a glint in the same position in each eye.

The finished eyes.

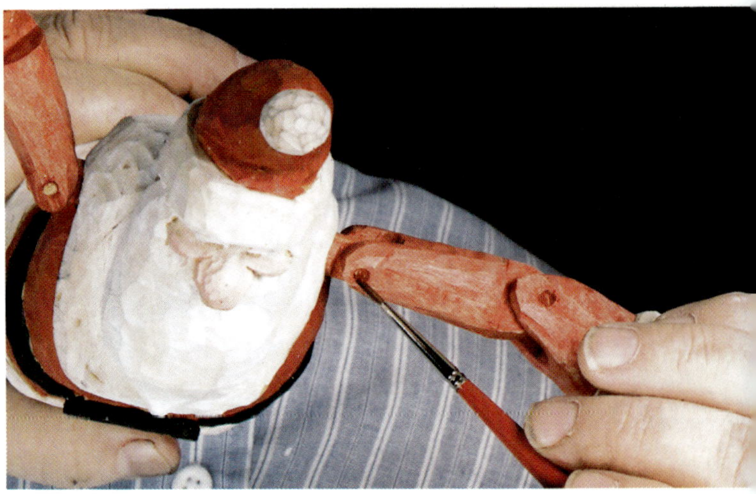

Two finishing touches. First, touch up the pegs with red paint.

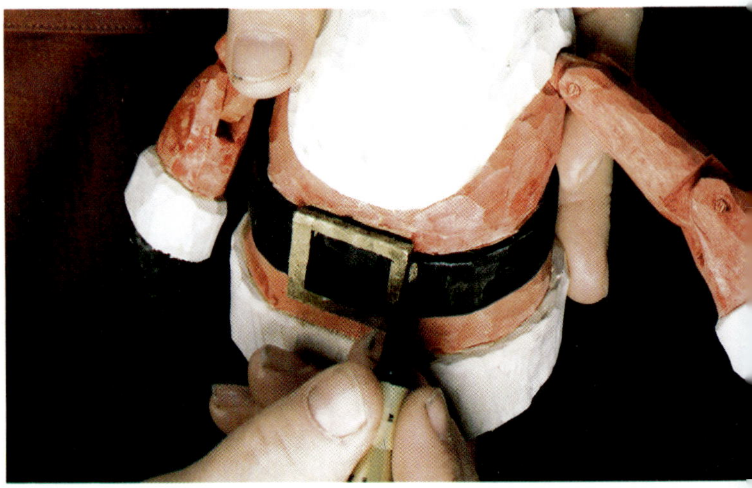

Second, use a gold pen to brighten up the belt buckle.

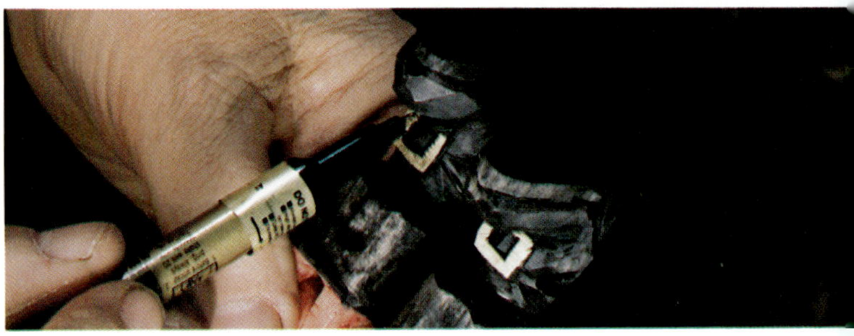

Continue with the gold on the shoe buckle.

The finished Santa.

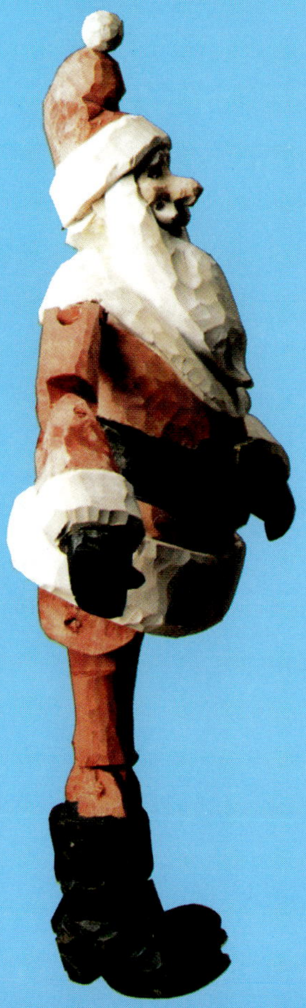

The Gallery

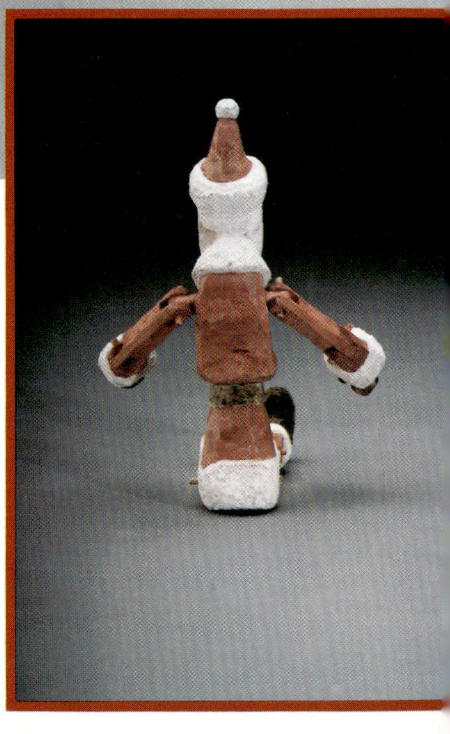

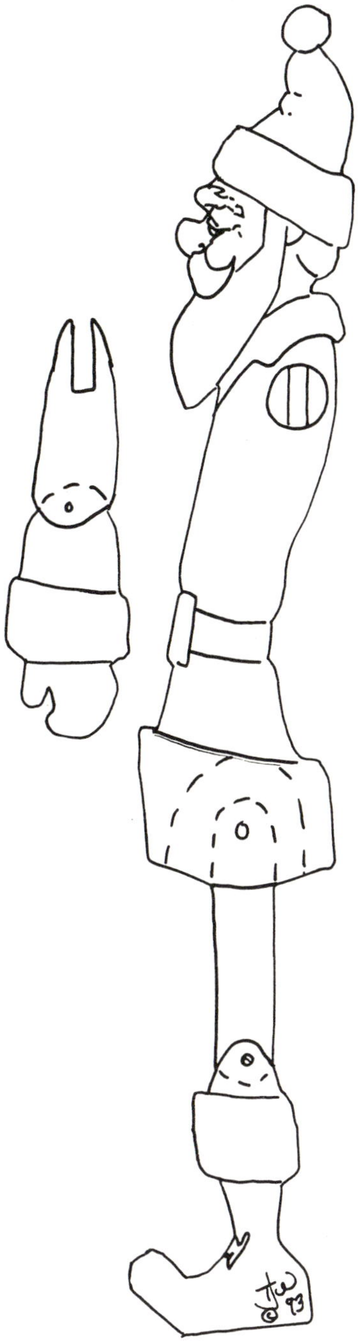

The pattern is shown at 66% of its actual size. If you wish to restore it to its original size, photocopy at 150%.

The pattern is shown at 66% of its actual size. If you wish to restore it to its original size, photocopy at 150%.

The pattern is shown at 66% of its actual size. If you wish to restore it to its original size, photocopy at 150%.

The pattern is shown at 66% of its actual size. If you wish to restore it to its original size, photocopy at 150%.

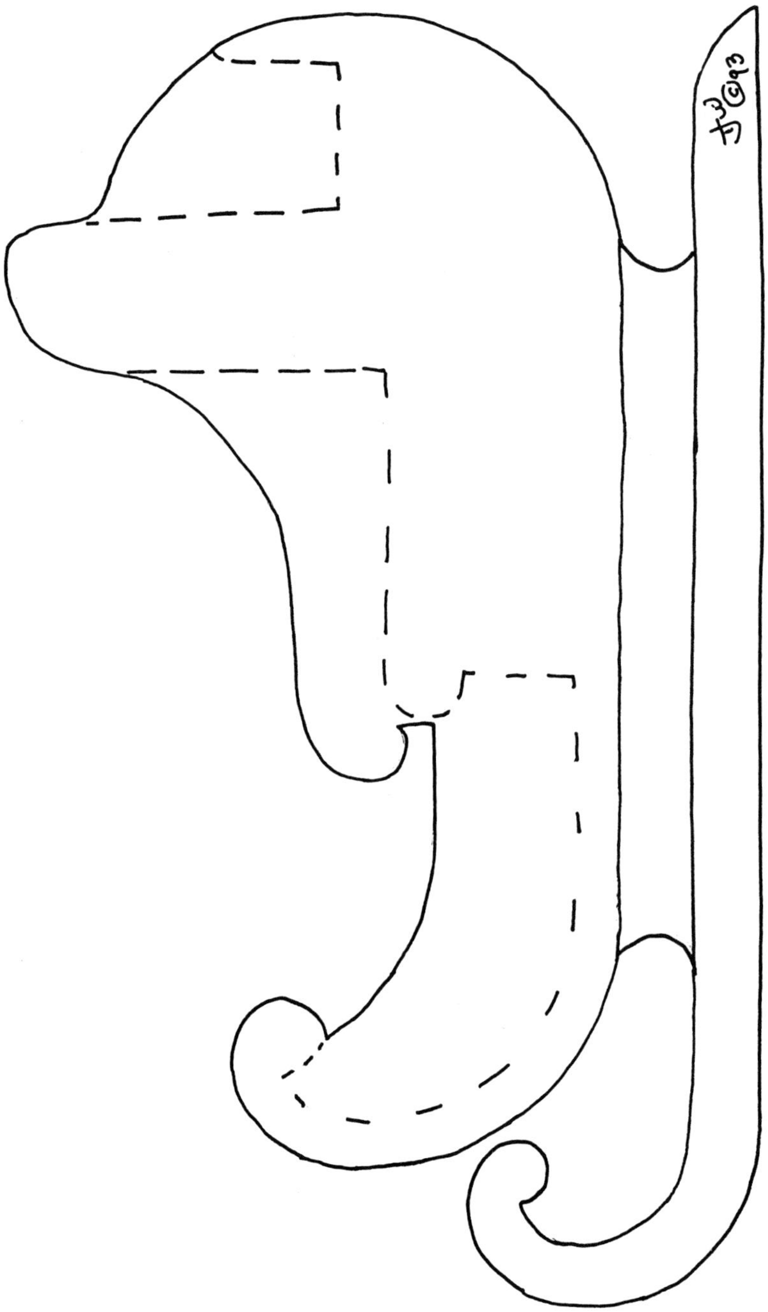

The pattern is shown at 66% of its actual size. If you wish to restore it to its original size, photocopy at 150%.

The pattern is shown at 66% of its actual size. If you wish to restore it to its original size, photocopy at 150%.

The pattern is shown at 66% of its actual size. If you wish to restore it to its original size, photocopy at 150%.

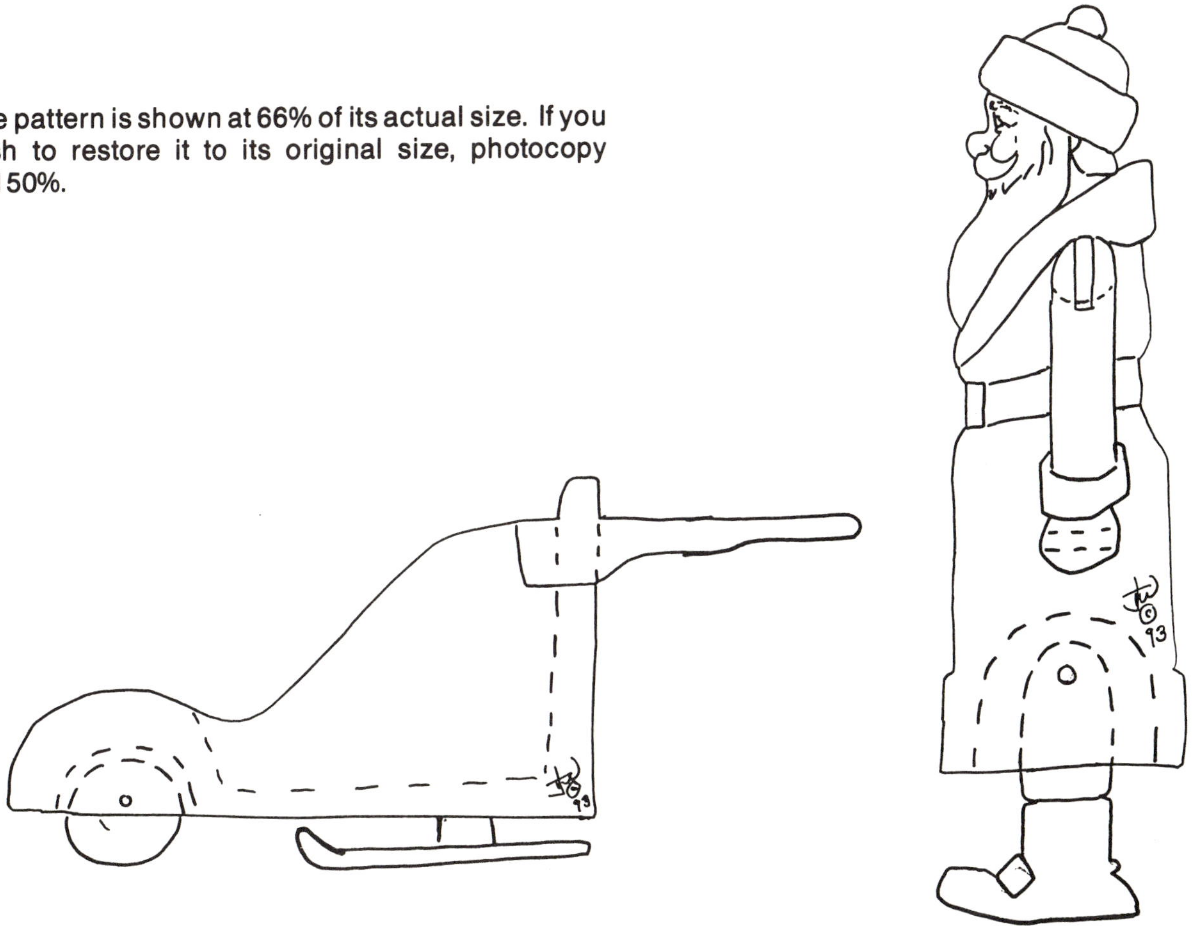

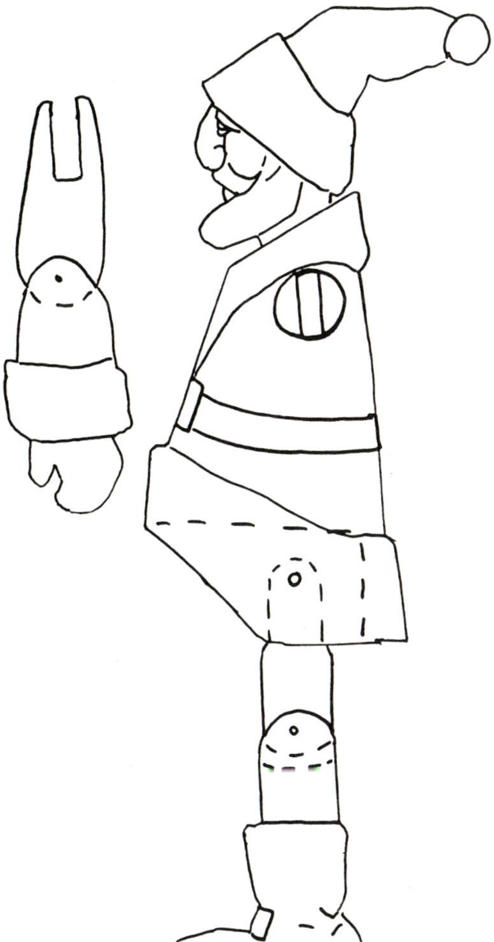

The pattern is shown at 66% of its actual size. If you wish to restore it to its original size, photocopy at 150%.

The pattern is shown at 66% of its actual size. If you wish to restore it to its original size, photocopy at 150%.

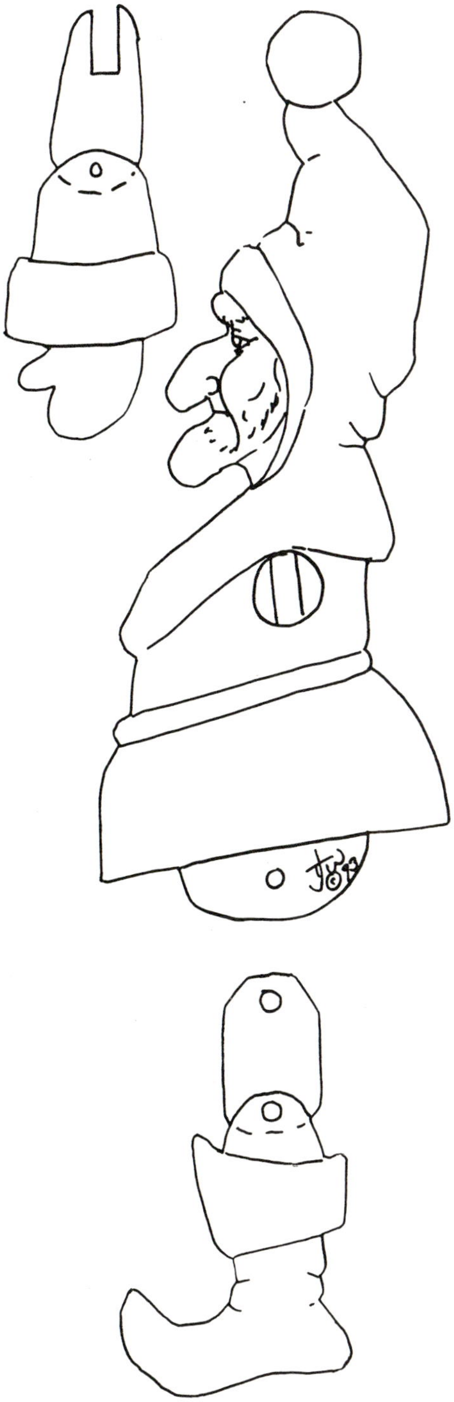